The Seven

Chakra Sisters

THE SEVEN
CHAKRA SISTERS

Make Friends with the
Inner Allies Who Keep
You Healthy, Laughing,
Loving, and Wise

LINDA LINKER ROSENTHAL

HAMPTON ROADS

Cover art © masevich/shutterstock
Interior designed by Jane Hagaman

Hampton Roads Publishing Company, Inc.
Charlottesville, VA 22906
Distributed by Red Wheel/Weiser, LLC
www.redwheelweiser.com

Sign up for our newsletter and special offers by going to:
www.redwheelweiser.com/newsletter.

ISBN: 978-1-57174-692-4

Library of Congress Cataloging-in-Publication Data available upon request

Printed on acid-free paper in the United States of America
MAL

10 9 8 7 6 5 4 3 2 1

For all of us . . . and our team of inner allies.

Knowing others is intelligence; knowing yourself is true wisdom. Mastering others is strength; mastering yourself is true power.

—LAO TZU, *TAO TE CHING*

Your living is determined not so much by what life brings to you as by the attitude you bring to life; not so much by what happens to you as by the way your mind looks at what happens.

—KAHLIL GIBRAN

Contents

Acknowledgments   xiii

Introduction   xv

Part I

1   The Septuplets Arrive   1

2   The Naming Ceremony   5

3   The Spiral Staircase   17

4   1st Floor, Aneeda: The Grounded Sister—I Need   19

5   2nd Floor, Ivanna: The Sensual Sister—I Want   23

6   3rd Floor, Ahafta: The Motivated Sister—I Have To   30

7   4th Floor, Ahluvya: The Loving Sister—I Love   36

8   5th Floor, Singya: The Expressive Sister—I Tell It Like It Is 41

9   6th Floor, Useeme: The Intuitive Sister—I See Everything   47

10   7th Floor, Iamone: The Spiritual Sister—I Am One   53

11   Queenking: The Androgynous Generator
     on the Highest Level—I Witness   57

12   The Fundalini's Visit   59

13   Meanwhile, Back on the Top Floor—
     The Manifesting Journey Begins   63

14   The Journey Back Up the Castle Again—
     The Sisters Are Getting the Hang of It   67

15   A Grand Festival—
     The Seven Chakra Sisters Work as a Team   73

16   A Secret Ceremony Takes Place—
The Chakra Sisters Have Sweet Memories   77

17   The Festival Flows As It Comes and Goes—
All Is Well in Thisismeville   86

18   Sweet Dreams for the 7 Chakra Sisters—
Or Is It a Nightmare?   89

Part II

19   A Mysterious Virus on Mt. Iknowmenow—
Forgetfulness Descends   91

20   The Spell of Fear—
Aneeda Encounters Fergetcha Kundameanie   93

21   The Spell of Guilt—Ivanna Is Enticed   98

22   The Spell of Self-Doubt—Ahafta's Fires Are Extinguished   103

23   The Spell of Worry—Ahluvya's Heart Gets Broken   106

24   The Spell of Dishonesty—Singya Loses Her Voice   109

25   The Spell of Confusion—Useeme Is Blindsided   112

26   The Spell of Boredom—Iamone's Lights Go Out   115

27   The Spells Take Hold—The 7 Chakra Sisters
Forget Their Natural State of Being   118

28   There's Dissention in the Castle—A Precursor to Dis-ease   126

29   Ahluvya Worries—
The Separation Starts from the Center Floor   129

30   Iamone Forgets Who She Is—
There's a Dangerous Disconnect on the Seventh Floor   131

31   Useeme Can't Make a Decision on the 6th Floor—
Her Third Eye Gets Blurry   133

32   Singya Is Feeling Bad Vibes on the 5th Floor—
"Why Won't They Listen?"   135

33 The Heart of the Crystal Castle Weakens—
Ahluvya's Health Is in Decline 137

34 There's Trouble on the 3rd Floor—
Ahafta Becomes Compulsive 138

35 The Castle Slips and Slides—
Ivanna Forgets How to Go with the Flow 140

36 The Foundation Is in Danger—
Aneeda Becomes Needy and Loses Her Footing 144

37 The Castle Is Collapsing—Singya Becomes Desperate ... 147

38 The Dis-ease on Mt. Iknowmenow Is Contagious—
Thisismeville Is in Conflict 151

Part III

39 The Royal Parents Finally Wise Up—
Don't Just Witness, Do Something! 153

40 Owl Woman Returns—To the Rescue 156

41 A Message Is Revealed—The Healing Begins 160

42 The Sacred Fire Is Lit—
Will the 7 Chakra Sisters Remember Themselves? 169

43 Mom and Dad Start Breathing Heavy—
And There's Nothing Sexy About It 195

44 It Rests on Aneeda—Remembering Who's Who 198

45 A Final Encounter with Fergetcha Kundameanie 207

46 One More Important Choice for the 7 Chakra Sisters ... 221

Glossary **227**

Acknowledgments

My deepest gratitude goes first to my favorite storyteller—my dad, Bob Linker, for teaching me how to sharpen my brain by using humor and word games with a quick wit. And to my mother, Bea, who put up with our nightly lobbing of puns across the dinner table as I was growing up, often having to excuse herself because she was laughing so hard. Thank you for birthing me. I love you both!

Thank you God, for blessing me always, in all ways, especially for my joy-filled children and their families who are resilient and brilliant—Brian, Jen, Jenny, Michael, Jodi, Steve, Lisa, Stu, Jacob, Lyla, Dena, Marc, Joshua, Gabby, and my amazing crystal granddaughter Roxie who, like her dad, has her own weird way with words.

I have also been blessed with wise teachers everywhere who have opened the doors to my imagination: authors, wisdom keepers, and storytellers—Clarissa Pinkola Estes, Lynn Andrews, Julia Cameron, Osho, and Lao Tzu; evocators and visionaries—Jean Houston, Barbara Marx Hubbard, and Bruce Lipton; and soul teachers who validated my inner knowings—Kahlil Gibran, Sri Aurobindo, Neale Donald Walsch, Michael Beckwith, Marianne Williamson, and Don Miquel Ruiz. Thank you to the educators who enlightened and impassioned my initial understanding of the chakras—Cyndi Dale, Anodea Judith, Ambika Wauters, Alan Seale—and the teachers and healers at Delphi who brought transformational RoHun™ healing into my life. Thank you Yvonne and Laurelle for initiating me into the art of Reiki. I humbly and respectfully thank you all for sharing your knowledge, wisdom, and experiences so others can awaken.

I want to acknowledge the teachers who have no names but have given me endless moments of inspiration, support, and encouragement—Grandmother Tree, the family of owls who talked to me over the course of one mystical summer, Panther medicine, spirit guides, celestial beings and angels who transmit insights while they visit my dream states, and the intuitive voice that expressed itself as God on the pages of my journals. And, of course, my seven chakra sisters, who do have names now!

My appreciation goes to all the clients, students, friends, healers, lightworkers, and circles of wise women who have come into my life for the past eighteen years and still show me the meaning of unconditional love every day. You know who you are.

I have immense gratitude for this new adventure with my Hampton Roads Publishing team. Randy Davila, Caroline Pincus, Addie Johnson, and Vanessa Ta, thank you for believing in me and helping birth the seven chakra sisters into the world. This might never have happened without Liz Dawn and the Mishka Productions family, who gave me the opportunity to grow and share my purpose by teaming up Celebrate Your Life with Hampton Roads to offer a writers workshop and contest in the summer of 2011. I am forever grateful to you. This book is the result of following my intuition and saying yes to what might be possible. It was beshert (destined)! I also want to acknowledge the new writer friends I met in Phoenix who continue to give me the courage to break through my fears and embrace the process. Thank you for holding that sacred space for me Eric, Elmdea, Jayelle, and Marilyn.

Finally, I am in awe of my soul's eternal wisdom which is guiding me to gracefully maneuver through this human experience on earth. Thank you for loving me.

My heart knows there are many more who I haven't mentioned, but I'm as complete as I can be for now—except to thank *you*, readers, for coming into my life to meet the seven chakra sisters. *We* appreciate you the most!

Introduction

On a muggy August day many summers ago I was particularly distraught about the negative energies that were consuming my household with three young, active children and a husband whose health was spiraling downhill with his addiction to pain medicine. I locked myself into my room and privately prayed onto the blank pages of my journal, asking for help—no, screaming for help!

I used my pen as a mighty beacon of light, sending a query out into the universe for my guardian angel to appear . . . or my spirit guide . . . someone or something who would simply introduce themselves to me and let me know that I was not alone. I had known since I was a child that God was always with me, but I wanted something more immediate. It makes me laugh to say that now.

My prayers were answered in a way that I least expected. As I wrote, I kept hearing, "team of seven." That's all. "Team of seven." This was very confusing. Seven what? Seven days of the week? Seven letters in my recently deceased grandfather's name, Solomon? The seven dwarfs? Was I so blessed as to actually have seven guardian angels? Names, please! But nope, just "team of seven."

My healing journey took many twists and turns to finally get me to see that I was the one with the problem. I needed healing as much as anyone with an addiction. I was asleep. I could not see or recognize that the spell of dis-ease was not only consuming my husband, it was also killing my whole family and me as well. As I continued to seek help through various holistic therapies, I was eventually introduced to the concept of the chakra system.

Chakra is an ancient Sanskrit word that means "spinning wheel," or "wheel of light." The chakras, or energy centers of the body, according to Western science, function as points along the spinal cord that process chemical and electromagnetic information between the cells. The location of each chakra corresponds to a particular part of the endocrine system, which manufactures the hormones that stimulate the cells into action.

But it is the more esoteric and metaphysical understanding of these energy vortices that interests me the most! The chakras are interdependent emanations of light and consciousness that each has its own color, shape, and intensity determined by their movement and rate of spin (frequency). Information from the world around us enters through the chakras. Likewise, energy and information from within us are also sent forth into the world from the chakras.

As part of my healing practice I did standing yoga poses in front of my colorful chakra banner to keep my physical body strong during those years of my family's challenges. I began to learn how the energy that kept me alive and functioning came through these seven spinning portals that corresponded to every internal organ system of my anatomy, even though the chakras are not a physical form. It wasn't until years later that it hit me. *That* was my Team of Seven! My seven energy portals, or chakras. They were the team that would help me heal! Why hadn't I realized it sooner?

I found out that whatever I was thinking or feeling, whether positive or negative, the chakras energized those thoughts and emotions even more. That truth manifested when I secretly wished for my husband to just go away, leave our home and get into a rehab center. Whenever I had fearful thoughts of losing money, or felt insecure from a lack of trust, my tailbone would scream in pain, signaling that my root chakra's energy was corresponding to my foundation and sense of personal safety. I learned that the energy in my first chakra was dense and heavy, which blocked the life force from flowing easily through me. Metaphorically and metaphysically I had a hard time moving forward in life. Whenever I stifled my voice, withholding any meaningful conversation in my relationship, I developed a throbbing ache in my neck and shoulders, which meant that my throat chakra was closing down its energy. I couldn't express myself and found that I was not only shutting up my ability to speak up for myself, but that my body was also shutting down, and my health suffered for it.

Through my later work with energy as a metaphysician and transpersonal psychologist, I discovered how our thoughts create our emotions by the amount of energetic information circulating through our chakras. We might feel a range of physical sensations, from sluggishness to hyperactivity, depending on how congested or scattered this energy might be. Our emotional states can be calm or turbulent, and our mental body might be very clear or become confused. All of these varied states are created from our immediate thoughts and belief systems which cascade the energy of either fear or love throughout our body, mind, and heart. When we feed ourselves loving thoughts, our chakras expand, allowing more life force to energize our vitality, which translates to good health. On the other hand, negative and fearful thoughts cause our chakras to respond by slowing their vibrational spin, causing uncomfortable feelings and dis-ease.

I couldn't get away from them, my team of seven who lived inside of me. I learned how the chakras awakened my spiritual connection through meditating on them. Now, I know them as my amazing friends and I meditate with them! They are always with me, helping, healing, and guiding me through life. Actually, they are the master keys to living my life fully, and they are as immediate as God is inside of me.

Eventually, wholeness returned. A sad divorce ended thirty years of marriage, and exactly one year later, the father of my children died. To keep my own sanity and health, I continued my studies of holistic healing, finding that these seven little chakra friends kept popping up all the time to keep me on track. It seems like they knew that I might sink into a deep and endless depression if I didn't keep moving forward.

These seven lovable characters who I call my "chakra sisters" are unique, and it is my hope that you will relate to each of them in your own way as your inner brothers, sisters, or simply your best friends! You will find archetypal, universal qualities in each of them that you might recognize in yourself, and I hope you will let them help you see yourself with a new, higher perspective. After all, the sisters represent our energy body, which determines our consciousness and overall health and well-being.

Although chakras are referred to as "subtle energy" by those in the field of mind-body medicine, these seven chakra sisters were not so subtle with me; they found very mischievous ways of getting my attention. When I was in need of healing from my codependency, I kept noticing how often I spoke of "needing" things, like more trust or security. The foundation of my safe home life seemed to be crumbling under the weight of addictive behaviors from my husband. My needs were not being met. Each time I said "I need . . . (a new life, a way to make more money, a friend who listens, etc.)," the root chakra sister, Aneeda, introduced herself. Eventually, each chakra sister's specific name revealed a psychological component which showed me how I was functioning. Was I being needy? (*Aneeda*) Was I wanting valuable or frivolous things? (*Ivanna*) Was I being honest and responsible with myself? Was I motivated enough to make some changes in my life? (*Ahafta*) Was I being compassionate, loving, and forgiving? (*Ahluvya*) Was I expressing myself truthfully? (*Singya*) Was I following the voice of my intuition and seeing myself clearly? (*Useeme*) Was I connecting with my spiritual essence, or was my ego running the show? (*Iamone*)

When the seven chakra sisters showed me their best qualities, I was able to know and identify with them in an even more personal way. Understanding each of the chakra sisters helped me better understand my own thoughts and emotions. They became my powerful healing team and helped me remember my Higher Self. This is how the book you are holding came to be born. They wanted you to also meet who is living inside of *you*.

I am a storyteller—I have filled more than thirty journals with real-life adventures of drama, trauma, and boredom. In fact, they were not journals—they were two-inch-thick sketchbooks, all handwritten with more questions than answers, until the inner wisdom eventually surfaced, bringing insights that transformed my life. When my children were young, we spent endless hours telling make-believe stories at bedtime to inspire creative or peaceful dreams. I have had in-depth conversations with ancient trees, and I teach what I need to learn for myself in classes such as chakra studies, energy mastery, meditation, and intuitive journaling. All along, my chakra sisters were being activated, and they inspired me with their humor and imagination when I most needed to lighten up. In this book, the chakra sisters and I are teaming up through the art of storytelling to mix a little fact with a lot of fantasy. Our hope is to teach as well as entertain you in a lighthearted way so you can get acquainted with the personalities of your chakras. With this book, you can make friends with your own seven inner energy allies who are eager to assist you on an adventurous healing journey toward health, happiness, love, and wisdom.

In this book, I bridge Eastern mysticism with Western psychology to illustrate that chakras are intelligent energy that bring a heightened intuitive awareness to our spiritually human experience. If you are already familiar with the chakra system and have worked with chakra healing in some way, you will find that *The Seven Chakra Sisters* can give you a new understanding of one of the most urgent issues facing humanity today: our free-will choice to cooperate within and without for personal and planetary healing and peace.

The health of our planet first begins with our own personal health. In the story, the chakra sisters inhabit a crystal castle, which is a metaphor for our miraculous human body. This includes not only our physical body, but also our mental, emotional, and spiritual body, which are all equal components of the whole. When all of the seven chakra sisters are working in harmony inside of us, then the castle of our body, mind, heart, and soul is at peace. The castle functions well when the chakra sisters create a healthy overall inner environment. When all the sisters are getting along together—for example, by eating wisely, avoiding stress, exercising to stimulate and cleanse the body and mind, practicing unconditional love, getting proper sleep, and being mindful—it naturally makes us feel good. Our optimal health comes to us when we allow these seven sisters to do what they each do best in a synergistic way.

On the other hand, the flow of our vital energy can be blocked by fearful thoughts which can create negative emotions. This happens when the seven chakra sisters are not communicating clearly with each other. If they forget their original divine essence because of their own or other's judgments or misguided mental and emotional programming, then there will surely be a breakdown in the castle. The spell of forgetfulness shows us how disease can manifest when we lose the memory of our oneness, our true spiritual essence, our soul's wisdom, God-consciousness, or whatever you choose to call the truth of your being. Each chakra sister's development of consciousness depends upon the others, and they must learn to work together to bring harmony to the entire castle. Each individual castle is a microcosm of the whole community.

When we listen to the guiding intuitive voice of our chakra sisters, we can bring peace into our world wherever we go. The seven chakra sisters teach us how to make conscious choices that benefit our own crystal castles on all levels. Just as the chakras need to work together to have a healthy body, each healthy person can choose to work in harmony with other people to help all of humanity evolve gracefully toward a new world of peace. From that higher, healthy perspective we can see ourselves as cooperative, loving, and spiritually mature planetary beings.

I hope this story resonates in every reader's heart to remind us how important it is to finally end the inner conflicts of our ego that live in the paradigm of separateness. This is a story about healing and returning to wholeness. The seven chakra sisters guide us to fully embrace the essence of our integrated, awakened Self with forgiveness and love. Once we are awake and aware of our true Authentic Selves, we can easily and effortlessly be healthy, happy, loving, and wise. Only in this state of being can we experience true inner peace, and our radiant crystal castle body can shine!

1
The Septuplets Arrive

O nce upon an ancient time, when all conditions were aligned with Mother Nature's wisdom, a magnificent crystal castle grew from the rocks and earth of a towering mountain called Mt. Iknowmenow, in the enchanted land of Thisismeville.

Mother Queen and Father King lived at the highest pinnacle of this crystal castle in a floating penthouse hovering just above the majestic mountaintop. They acted as one, so evolved were they, and they were often referred to as the Queenking.

Owl Woman paced over rough stones on the precipice of the mountain in anticipation, her white feathers flying out in small tufts of fluff as her large foot-talons gripped the shaking ground beneath her. "It is almost time! I can feel the rumblings right here on Mt. Iknowmenow! Finally! For eons, the royal crystal castle has been preparing for this moment. I am ready to assist the Queenking! Soon, she—I mean he—I mean *they* will be preoccupied with parenthood!"

Owl Woman, a magical being on Mt. Iknowmenow who carried the essence of a winged one with human attributes, was known as a wise and lovable character. While wringing her bird-hands with expectancy, a great blaring of trumpets issued forth, signaling the momentous event. The blasts of sound catapulted her into flight as she screeched, "Wait! Wait for meeeeeee! I am the frequency holder, the earth and starseed medicine woman. You can't start without me!"

The townspeople from the nearby village of Thisismeville quickly gathered to hear the news. Something extraordinary was happening in the castle. It was another step in the evolution of humanity! The celebration was so joyous that Mother Earth shook every leaf and the skies broke open to bursts of golden rays.

Swooping through the pink quartz doors of the crystal castle, Owl Woman took her place with the Queenking's ancient lineage of advanced sages, healers, alchemists, shamans, energy masters, and wisdom keepers.

A royal family event such as this happened on Mt. Iknowme-now whenever the settled and accepted way of life in Thisismeville needed a change. Everyone in the queendom was ready for a quantum leap in consciousness. This moment was too precious to experience from a distance, and Owl Woman wanted a front row seat. She was determined to be present with an appropriate bird's eye view.

She spread her wings like elbow plowshares and pushed her way through the adoring crowd. "Let me through . . . please excuse me . . . coming through, please . . . move aside now!" All were there to welcome the birth of the newborn princess septuplets.

Owl Woman made sure that she was the first to touch the crowns of their glistening heads. The contact immediately lifted her feathers up, covering her with a blanket of owlbumps. "Energia! Welcome! My little darling way-showers, you have no idea how powerful you are yet! I have so much to teach you. I can't wait to get started!"

It was an honored guest at the welcoming celebration—the inner energy sage of the Far East—who acknowledged right away that the seven royal newborns each carried a circular energy which swirled inside and around their tiny bodies at their own particular speed and color. At that time, no one but the energy sage and Owl Woman could decipher their individual distinguishing characteristics.

Clearing his throat, the sage spoke slowly and deliberately, stringing out his *s*'s in long notes of emphasis, enunciating like an aged linguistics professor, "I now proclaim . . . that the gyrating energy vorticessss which emanate from thesssse newborns'ssss colorful electromagnetic fieldssss . . . ssshall be called . . . chakrasssss!"

A polite chorus of *ooohs* and *ahhhs* were accompanied by gentle clapping so as to not disturb the babies.

Owl Woman chimed in next. "These chakras look like adorable little spinning wheels, though you can't see them," she said, ignoring the fact that many of the guests surrounding the babies were also masters of metaphysics who could easily see the active movement of the newborns' energy fields.

Feeling quite proud that she was chosen to be the children's godmother, Owl Woman continued with a bit of drama to just slightly upstage the sage. "I proclaim . . . for these precious seven chakra princess sisters . . . that the *speed* of the *spin* of these invisible wheels shall match the *aliveness* and *vitality* of their *consciousness!*"

Nods of approval and more soft applause filled the spacious foyer of the castle.

The septuplets arrived as the newest bodhisattvas, or wise teachers, knowing their journey was to come back to Earth to shine a light on others so they would see their own greatness. Entering the earth plane for the first time, the sisters were tiny in body but huge in spiritual memory. They knew they had work to do and welcomed it as the joy of their purpose, later learning that *living on purpose* was the purpose for their joy.

The story keepers chanted homage to their radiance, and collectively the seven sisters were imbued with a sound that translated as "Beautiful Oneness." It was the kind of beauty that flowed from their tiny infant bodies in streams of Technicolor energy waves, touching everything around them, from the nearest healing hands to the vast infinite space of the great expanse.

The celebration continued as Spiderwoman began weaving a soft cradle of luminous silken threads for each chakra sister. Archangels watched over them and cooed in subliminal languages that spoke of the new babies' intuitive powers. Black Panther came and offered himself as their first animal totem, paying homage by pacing slowly around the princesses three times, creating a circle of everlasting protection. These seven special children already knew how to shine their eternal lights with skill and grace even at birth. They accepted their gifts with deep love and gratitude, so advanced were their boundless souls. The little ones dazzled the castle with their powerful life force.

Even from a great distance, way out in the Thisismeville countryside, people could see a brilliant light emanating from the crystalline castle high atop the mountain.

"Look! Each floor of the castle is shimmering in its own colorful glow!"

"Amazing! Our Queenking's crystal mansion is enchanting now that the seven little princesses have arrived!"

In the years following the royal birth, the townspeople could always tell if the kingdom was running smoothly by how brightly the castle lights were shining.

The Beautiful Ones brought great happiness to Thisismeville, and all the townspeople collectively sighed. Their hearts opened wide to the new additions in their village.

For the next seven days Owl Woman circled above the mountain, keeping vigil over the baby sisters. Centering herself in the palpable love from the crystal castle, Owl Woman gushed with pride over every step taken by the blessed family on this sacred ground.

2
The Naming Ceremony

Mother Queen and Father King prepared for their baby daughters' naming ceremony. It was tradition that on the seventh day after a royal baby's arrival, her spiritual name was to be revealed. The appointed guardian, in this case the ancient and wise Owl Woman, was to draw the seven chakra sisters' names directly from the Queenking's ancient cedar chest, where everything bore the lasting scent of cosmic and ancestral memory. Sometimes the royal familial chest emitted a peculiar smell as old as the fossilized mossy forests on Mt. Iknowmenow. Sometimes the fragrances were as fresh as the apple blossoms in the kingdom's spring gardens. On the rare occasion that called for the age-old trunk to be opened, the odor was a sign to be prepared for the unexpected.

Owl Woman opened the trunk, and the sacred fragrances of myrrh and frankincense filled the room. She reached down deep into the bottomless chest with crooked hands that resembled tree bark and raw amethyst wands. As she rooted around, touching each name with tender understanding, smells of the salty ocean, damp black earth, and galaxy dust wafted out.

She felt the profound titles that would saturate each sister with their proper frequency. One by one, she let the essences roll slowly between her palms. Closing her huge, knowing eyes, Owl Woman held each name to her heart until seven designations evoked the strongest impressions. Each name carried a specific vibration which rippled through the enchanted crystal castle and throughout the land.

Owl Woman knew that together these vibrant beings would carry the memory and information necessary to awaken all the inhabitants of Thisismeville. Slowly and deliberately, while tapping each tiny child on the crown of her head with knobby fingers, Owl Woman lovingly spoke the seven precious names out loud for the first time. Aneeda... Ivanna... Ahafta... Ahluvya... Singya... Useeme... and Iamone.

Owl woman turned to the first child and said in a resonant tone of prophecy, "Aneeda, your strong legs will be a stable foundation on the ground floor of the crystal castle. You will learn to plant and anchor your life energy deeply into Mother Earth to keep yourself and all your sisters centered and connected to all of life."

Holding Aneeda's infant feet with firm resolve, Owl Woman spoke a bit louder now. "My little rooter, you hold the key to igniting the energy in the entire castle. You are the gatekeeper for the life force to rise up to the upper floors of the castle. You must have the ability to feel secure, even during times of stress and change. You will encounter challenges, but you must continue to trust that all of your needs will be met and that you are always safe in a world of abundant sustenance. You must be steadfast and well grounded on the first floor, Aneeda, or the entire castle may crumble and fall! All of your sisters will be depending on you for good health, so keep your focus on the everlasting value of your family and your life."

There was a long silence before Aneeda gave a little shudder of acknowledgment for her blessing.

Next, Owl Woman took the second sister's hands and placed them low upon her tiny abdomen. Holding her around her flexible little hips, Owl Woman said, "You will carry the name of Ivanna, my little intense, juicy child! Your emotional states will govern all of your relationships. Your moods will determine how well all your sisters get along with each other. Be aware of your changing temperament, and always remember that you must cooperate with others—especially with your sisters. When you honor all of your feelings and emotions, Ivanna, most of all your natural state of joy, the flowing waters of your sweet sensuality will help you move through any obstacle."

At this point Owl Woman's smile shifted and her eyes squinted a bit. "Ivanna, heed my warning to be very mindful of your many wants and desires! You will want, want, want your world to be all about you, and it is . . . but you must remember that it's also *not* about you at all! Your job is to establish healthy relationships with others. When you generously share yourself, the whole castle will benefit with pleasure."

Ivanna wiggled her little hips to loosen Owl Woman's grip as her godmother continued, "Your gift of clairsentience will give you the ability to feel and sense what other people are feeling and sensing. Know what is yours and what belongs to others, little empathic one!

Owl Woman sighed deeply and sent extra love to Ivanna, knowing how this little princess would need to mature to keep the castle flowing and growing.

"Never underestimate the powerful force of the vroom-vroom energy that you carry within you. Just as the power of water can both nourish life and drown it to death, do not overstep your bounds with that emotional power on the second floor!" Ivanna squirmed a bit more and then gave Owl Woman a tiny mischievous wink.

Unruffled, Owl Woman moved on, rubbing the next chakra sister on her tummy as she spoke. "Ahafta, sweet sunshine, you will establish your powerful solar energy on the third floor of the castle. You will be in charge of all the elements of fire in the castle and beyond. Remember, little brilliant jewel, that fire can warm and transform . . . but it can also destroy everything in its path. Use your individual fire energy wisely. It will give you the courage and motivation to believe in yourself and burn through the ego's self-doubt.

"You have the gift of control, but only of your own energy. You might feel like you have to control things, situations, and even manipulate other people, but stay focused on your own personal power—no one else's. Your concern will be learning to establish a strong relationship with yourself. Self-honesty and integrity will be the keys to your high self-esteem." Ahafta gazed up into Owl Woman's eyes and pursed her young pink lips with a shiver of determination.

"There is one more important message for you, my golden roaring-fire child. Your two little sisters who live on the floors below you will have a strong pull of gravity. You will have to stoke your fires to help pull Aneeda up out of inertia and to guide Ivanna from flitting about too much. You will be the one who can bring them up to the heart of the castle so the three of you can enter into the heart of love."

Ahafta was feeling her sense of personal responsibility expanding inside her solar plexus. She placed her tiny hands over Owl Woman's and they rubbed her midsection in one circular swirl.

Owl Woman was halfway through the naming ceremony and was getting more energized with each radiant being of light. She turned toward the next sister, knowing that Aneeda, Ivanna, and Ahafta would need the loving energy of Ahluvya to pull them even higher up the castle floors for their spiritual nourishment.

"Little Ahluvya, you open our hearts!" exclaimed the Owl Goddess of Wisdom as she slowly placed both of her healing hands on the front and back side of the fourth floor chakra princess. A stream of pink and teal green light poured out from the center of Ahluvya's tiny chest.

"Ahluvya, you will be the great compassionate balancer. From the middle floor of the castle, you will lift up everyone around you. Your electromagnetic vital energy will be the strongest of all your sisters, and I will gift you with the blossoming green lotus flower of love, which will guide your life every day. You carry the precious right to love and to be loved, so be extremely gentle with your heart."

"Listen closely now," said Owl Woman as she bent her head down to Ahluvya's chest. "Never ever allow the gripping illusions of separation, war, or conflict to enter your center. Ahafta will help you understand that you must always love yourself first before you can share your expansive heart with others. And Iamone will help you stay focused on your purpose of being the compassionate presence in the castle. You, Ahluvya, will be the guiding force that offers loving service in the world—but only with the cooperation of your team of sisters. This is important!"

"Your life's work, Ahluvya, is to learn and then teach your sisters how to love completely, without any conditions whatsoever. No conditions, judgments, or expectations shall ever diminish your true understanding of the heart of love! Your gift is the ability to open your heart to all things—people, animals, Mother Earth. Your generous spirit will be inclusive to all, and all of your loving relationships will develop out of your sense of joy."

Owl Woman stepped back and suddenly threw open her large jeweled cape, which momentarily transformed into giant wings and caused a rush of wind to sweep through the ceremonial space. "Love is love, Ahluvya, and you are the sister who will remind the others about the vast space of the heart, which can hold everything. It is the energy of your heart center which will heal everything if and when the time is needed. You hold the mastery and the mystery of love."

Softening her tone, Owl Woman continued, "Your elemental nature is air, which will give you a lightness of being. Feel the powerful, sweet energy of love that is penetrating you right now. Each breath you take will help you move beyond the everyday earthly concerns of your sisters on the three floors below you to reach the upper realms of sound, light, and spiritual awareness above you."

Pausing for a moment, Owl Woman knew there was an important teaching that must be imparted to Ahluvya. "Be very mindful of your breathing patterns and the effect on your own heart, Ahluvya, because just as air can be light and free, it can also create great storms and violent turbulence. You must be discerning in what you inhale and also what you exhale," she cautioned.

Having stated that, Owl Woman brightened her tone once again. "You will easily share your heart with others, little center point, and your job is to balance the castle's understanding from me-thinking to we-being. As you learn to bring cooperation into the castle, you will make it easier for all of your sisters to give love and receive love in a larger way. It will be a delicate dance, Ahluvya, but you are the bridge between the egoic needs and wants of the castle and the spiritual aspects of your sisters' higher collective purpose. It all comes together in the heart, where you live."

Owl Woman was pleased. In her grandmotherly way, she issued a warning for this middle sister too. "It's most imperative that you keep your energy active and not let your giving and receiving get out of balance, oh little one of love, or the entire castle as well as the whole kingdom might collapse!" Ahluvya's bright green eyes widened as she sucked in a very deep breath of understanding.

Owl Woman turned next to the fifth chakra sister. "Singya, although your living space on the fifth floor of the castle will be the smallest of any of the floors, you will hold a concentration of high spiritual energy there," she said while lightly tapping Singya's throat. "Your voice will bring harmony into the entire castle. I will give you your own special song, and you will find creative ways to sing it into the world."

With that, Owl Woman swooped Singya up in her arms and began to chant a mantra:

> *I am free . . .*
>
> *I am free . . .*
>
> *I am free to be me!*

Singya giggled and a delightful sound echoed throughout all seven floors of the castle. "Remember this song, Singya, for it will help you filter and purify every thought that comes to you from your sisters. Your job is to distill their many thoughts and make sense of them in the most creative and spiritual way. Ultimately, you will express the truth with love and compassion."

Before moving on, Owl Woman paused and contemplated one final blessing for the fifth chakra sister. "Lovely Singya, with the gift of clairaudience you will not only speak with the highest integrity but you will also have the gift of listening with the purest intentions. Your sharp intuitive skills will allow you to hear inner messages that your sisters on the floors below you might miss. Your resonant voice will guide your sisters to speak their truth with profound honesty. . . and that will bring the greatest freedom to the castle!" Singya opened her little mouth and rounded her lips as if she would belt out an operatic sound, but yawned out loud instead, making Owl Woman giggle.

Now, turning toward the sixth child, Owl Woman held her first two fingers gently but firmly on the child's forehead. A deep indigo hue passed between the two of them, and they were engulfed in the mist of a timeless dimension.

"Useeme," whispered Owl Woman, "your place on the sixth floor is the most important command and control center of the entire castle. You will be the sister responsible for all the intelligent workings inside. You must be mindful of all the thoughts and creative imagination in the castle, paying close attention to all of your sisters as one seamless fabric of knowledge. Your ideas will flow from your brilliant mind all the way through the whole castle. You will hold the vibrations of the highest inspiration possible for you and your sisters' well-being. Your floor will hold a circular, sacred, psychic chamber of colors, visions, light, and wisdom. Useeme, your home will be a fun kaleidoscope of originality and imagination, so please make sure to invite the girls up to visit you often!"

Owl Woman reflected for a moment on this wondrous welcoming ceremony for the royal sisters. "I know how important it is for each of you to have an authentic sense of self and to understand your own unique roles as you grow up in the castle. But this is most important, dear ones." Owl Woman looked at the bundle of seven babies and stared hard into their eyes, "You must learn to see yourselves as one unit that works together like a finely tuned orchestra. You need each other to thrive, and you must always work together. Useeme, your mind will keep everyone focused on this. So, my little brainchild, I shall give you the ultimate gift of intuition and clairvoyance to help your sisters see what they need to see."

Owl Woman then touched Useeme's forehead right between her little eyebrows and said, "I now implant a third eye into you, which will let you have the capacity to see everything, to see beyond the illusions and tricks of the mind. You will know all of your chakra sisters' true intentions. Nothing will be hidden from you!"

Like the current of a rushing and powerful underground river of life, Owl Woman felt a sudden rising wave of appreciation for each of the unique seven chakra princess sisters.

"Working deep within the inner mind," she continued to Useeme, "you will shine the light of understanding onto all of your sisters' experiences and show them what they cannot see for them-selves. You will envision what is possible for all because you will have the ability to see the ordinary as extraordinary."

Owl Woman was feeling her own heart beating faster now, knowing the immense responsibility that this sister would carry. She spoke softly now, "Useeme, there is something you must know about your living space on the sixth floor. There are two opposite sides on your floor that will need to work together, just like you will need to work together with all of your sisters. When your reason and logic become integrated with your limitless vivid imagination your pro-found insights will guide all of your sisters and harmony will prevail wherever you go. But you must think clearly, Useeme. Your thinking will manifest the reality and experiences in the whole castle!"

The ancient godmother had one last assertion for the sixth chakra child. "Useeme, I see you and you see me; and when you can see yourself completely, then you will see yourself in everyone and see everyone in you. I acknowledge that the vibration of your name will be the reflective light for the whole castle and, indeed, for the entire coordinated workings of Thisismeville."

At that moment, a low guttural sound came from deep within Useeme, acknowledging all that Owl Woman had just told her. A long, slow sound of *aauu-ooohh-mmm* poured out of the small child who would be in charge of observing and clarifying all the perceptions in the crystal castle. Mt. Iknowmenow shook with pleasure.

There was one last child left to be named, and Owl Woman approached her with deep respect and reverence. She gently lifted the baby onto a lavender lotus blossom with a thousand golden petals that unfolded into infinity. "Iamone, your name resonates with the highest consciousness of the entire castle: 'I am one.' When your sisters know they are one with you, then true peace will exist not only in the castle but also in the entire queendom. You, beautiful Iamone, live at the pinnacle of the castle, the point of connection with the All. I now gift you with the ability to take all the knowledge you will gain from your sisters' experiences and transform it into wisdom! You are the closest to the universal mind which will flow to you from your divine parents above. You are the quintessential radiant chakra sister at the highest level of spiritual and human development!"

Iamone exuded a serene and peaceful countenance on the top floor of the castle, where she would live in her most high place. There were no ceilings on the seventh floor, which left her wide open to the endless dimensions beyond space. In her transcendent state of being she knew she was one with everything in the vast universe. Like any big sister looking out for the younger ones, she would be the one who transmitted all the spiritual guidance from the Queenking to her sisters on the floors below her.

Owl Woman could hardly contain her exuberance at this point. Her voice rose as she stretched onto the tips of her toes and pronounced with a theatrical melody, "To all of your sisters below you, you are the top banana, the highest buzz, the queen bee, the utmost crowning point culmination of every step that your sisters will take on their upward path to enlightenment!"

Waving her hands wildly, Owl Woman exclaimed, "You, Iamone, are the alpha and the omega. You are the top drawer, the top dog, the top-notch enchilada, the be-all and end-all epitome of purposeful living!!"

Spinning with ecstatic delight, she continued, "Iamone, you are one with your source of mother-father love. You are one with all of creation! You are it, baby, the cat's pajamas! You are the one! Your consciousness rules! You know all there is to know in your castle, this world, the entire cosmos! Iamone, you are *one* with the Source of all Consciousness. You connect everything within the galactic realms!"

By this time, the castle was rocking from side to side from Owl Woman's gyrations. One moment more of the godmother's merry cavorting would have started an avalanche on the mountainside. Realizing her animated spirit, Owl Woman suddenly stopped spinning and screeching. Her breath began to slow, and a heavy silence fell as she gently smoothed her frantic feathers and regained her composure. Slightly embarrassed, she cleared her throat and slowly searched for the proper words.

"OK, I admit the foibles of the ego and the drama that can ensue. I admit that just now I became attached to the outcome of my naming ceremony. Little ones, do you see how quickly we can be thrown off-center by our labels, expectations, and personal yearnings? Yes, even I forgot for a quick moment who I am. I forgot to surrender my ego to the ultimate beauty and wisdom of the divine within me. I got a bit carried away with things, so I accept my little slip-up of forgetfulness as a great lesson for your benefit. Iamone, you will help us remember who we truly are when our egos get inflated, right?"

Iamone was not at all concerned about Owl Woman's antics or apologies and simply lay happily on her lotus blossom. She understood her blissful place of being witness to all that transpired. It was Iamone's nature to accept everything just as it was in each moment. Like her loving sister Ahluvya, Iamone had no judgments, opinions, attachments, or complaints about anything. She understood the many personalities that would be living under her in the castle, but from her vantage point she had the highest perspective on things and could easily embrace everything that was going on around her without being caught in the web of drama and trauma.

However, after all the tumult from their beloved teacher, the other six chakra sisters looked quizzically at one another. Aneeda, rising to the occasion, had her first chance to use her blessing of grounding. At the exact same moment of understanding, Iamone knew that this would be her first opportunity to spill her spiritual power into her siblings. Together, they instinctively knew how to guide the five sisters in between them.

Following Iamone and Aneeda's lead, each sister reached out to hold the others' tiny hands. This simple act shot a spark of vital energy through each of them. Iamone's knowings linked with Useeme's visions, which joined Singya's intuitive voice, which fit perfectly into Ahluvya's accepting heart, which moved into Ahafta's confidence, down into Ivanna's emotional sensuality, and it was all anchored to Aneeda's strong foundation.

In that moment of connection, all seven chakra sisters knew that they could settle down in peace no matter what clamorous energy might come from outer circumstances. In that instant they remembered everything. They remembered their divine origins of stardust. They remembered their ability to come back to Earth, centered, calm, composed, and stable. They remembered that they were one in the infinite sea of universal energy. They remembered that they were one perfect diamond, polished and cut with seven unique facets. All they needed to know they knew already. In a flash of understanding, the seven chakra sisters vowed to always stay connected with one another.

After a very long meditative pause in which she completely missed the instant and brilliant collective awakening of the seven chakra sisters, Owl Woman stretched her wings to gather the babies around her in a close circle. Coincidentally, she chose to complete the royal naming ceremony by speaking of remembering.

"Beautiful Ones, you are my mission, my purpose, my raison d'être! It is imperative that I instill in you these last and most important instructions for living: you must remain connected to your spiritual source at all times. Remember that you are never separated from Source. Never! You are my little starseeded children. You have been born from the substance of the universe from which everything is created perfectly. Not only is Iamone one with all, but each of you are one with Iamone. You are *One Being* of many lights. You must remember to stay connected to one another always!"

The babies yawned respectfully as they gave Owl Woman their full attention. She continued, "Even though each of you are unique and will provide your own special function to the workings of the castle, you must remember that you can only be efficient if you work together as a team. Together you are whole and complete. You were born into this castle as one divine being of individual lights. If you separate from one another, for any reason, the castle will not be able to survive. Always be mindful of one another, all seven of you! You are many, but you are *one!*"

The seven little chakra princess sisters smiled at one another, knowing that they were a large step ahead of their beloved mentor who was diligently trying to teach them about what they had already remembered. Owl Woman sighed, "You may hear my teachings over and over again throughout your existence until you no longer need reminding, but for now, I do believe I am complete. I have given you all that I have and all that you need."

Satisfied, Owl Woman slowly closed the ancient cedarwood chest. It didn't matter that it was way past their bedtime by now. In full gratitude for Owl Woman's blessings of the day, and all the lessons of remembering, the seven precious princesses finally drifted off to dreams of butterflies and ancient star systems. In the background of their minds, sounds of a cosmic chorus softly sang their names into the cool night air over Mt. Iknowmenow . . . *Aneeda . . . Ivanna . . . Ahafta . . . Ahluvya . . . Singya . . . Useeme . . . Iamone . . .*

3

The Spiral Staircase

In the days after the naming ceremony the castle clamored with jackhammers, buzzing drill bits, and grinding handsaws. The divine Mother Queen and Father King were in the throes of remodeling the castle for their precious septuplets. They had waited for thousands of millennia to build the master golden spiral staircases that would be the mode of communication between the sisters on each level, and now the competent hands of gifted relatives—energy artisans and spiritually advanced carpenters from the surrounding countryside—were piecing together the structures in a double helix form.

There were seven magical floors to the crystal castle, and as Owl Woman had foretold, each princess had a floor all her own. The golden staircases would reach from the ground to the top floor through the open foyer at the center of the crystal structure. One staircase was for the sisters to travel upward; the other was for their descent, to assure that the energy would move free and clear in both directions. In the center between the two spiraling staircases, a clear column of pure radiant light connected the ground floor to each of the others and traversed through the roof to the Queenking, who inhabited the etheric space just above Iamone's seventh floor abode. This column of light assured that life-giving energies would continually rise through the castle even when the princesses were sleeping.

Soon the golden staircases were complete, and time passed quickly as the newborns grew up. With every step on the spiral staircase, the children could feel a slight tickly prickle on the soles of their little bare feet. Giddy with laughter, they ran up and down, winding round and round, from Aneeda's ground floor all the way up to the top open space of Iamone's room. The castle had come to life with the energy that stirred everything within its transparent walls.

4
1st Floor, Aneeda:
The Grounded Sister—
I Need

The royal castle's crystal structure, like all crystals from earth, grew right out of the side of the magical mountain. Planetary wisdom chose this particular sturdy and massive east-facing mountainside as housing for the crystal castle, and this is where the chakra sisters would learn the ways of living and being on Earth. The sisters' infinite energy filled every space on the seven expansive floors and each one held their highest frequencies for the crystal castle to thrive. The vibrations from each floor could be felt throughout the kingdom.

It was perfectly normal for the seven sisters to live without a sense of physical boundaries since they were energy beings, limitless in every way. Having indoor forests, rivers, gardens, or waterfalls was a natural part of their chosen décor. They relished every aspect of adjusting to terra firma.

Aneeda lived on the entire first floor foundation of the crystal castle. Gravity was the predominant energy here, and Aneeda was the only sister in the family who was comforted by the heavy, slow feeling of being pulled down securely toward the ground. The thick, dense feeling on the first floor felt to her like a warm, cozy blanket.

Aneeda's floor naturally held the sweet and woodsy fragrances of cedarwood, patchouli, and cloves. Being the slowest and heaviest of all her sisters, the simple act of running made her feel exhilarated. When her sisters teased her for smelling a little too earthy, like a seasoned barnyard, Aneeda would shriek with laughter, then take off after them like a jackrabbit.

Aneeda had penetrating raven black eyes and sported a mane of dark, sleek hair that spilled down to her waist. When she skipped down her long red hallway her ponytail swished from side to side, showing off her vibrant and healthy energy. Like her sisters above her, she was given free rein to do whatever she pleased on her floor of the castle. Aneeda didn't ask for much more than her basic needs, but when she first began speaking for herself, the castle heard her requests loud and clear.

"I need stwawbewwies! Wed cherwwies! Wed watamewwon!" The color red made Aneeda feel most alive. When she surrounded herself with red frequencies, a tingling energy vibrated up her spine, which always gave her a burst of passion and love for life. When her lips finally learned how to curve out enough to form the letter r, this blossoming toddler ran through her home on the first floor screaming out her four favorite words: "Red! Rocks! Roots! Run!"

Aneeda took great pride in her physical strength and strong legs, which gave her a sturdy foundation as she grew into her young childhood. Supported by her flexible hips and knees, Aneeda walked, ran, and sometimes even danced outside every day, enjoying her wild, earthy stamina.

"Aneeda, you do love Mother Earth more than anything, don't you?"

"We've seen you sitting in your gardens, smothering your little face into that red hydrangea bush. You're so funny!" said her sisters, who admired Aneeda's strong sense of belonging to the earth. "Why do you do that?"

"So I can smell the flowers' messages for healing, why else? And if I lay my ear to the ground long enough, I can hear the crystals speaking to me, too! Did you know that rubies can remind us how limitless we are? And that having a chunk of smoky quartz in your room will help you have awesome dreams?"

"What else do your crystal-rocks teach you, Aneeda?" Her sisters were curious to understand how their little sister on the ground floor could feel so connected to nature, so they could too.

"Well, not that we would ever encounter any stress or negativity . . . but if we did, then black obsidian could help disperse that energy. But you might have to sit on it, or put some small hematite stones in your shoes."

"Black rocks in my chakra socks? No way!" laughed Ivanna.

Beyond the flowers, Aneeda could be found in the forests feeling dwarfed in size but trying as hard as she could to stretch her little arms all the way around the giant redwoods. She only needed to hug any tree near her to enliven her sense of belonging to the earth.

So strong was her love of nature, she found ways to bring the outside into the castle. Aneeda's floor housed indoor walking paths lined with red oak trees and accented with garnet tiles. Her recreation room was landscaped with live trees, flowers, shrubs, and russet wallpaper.

Sometimes, instead of being outdoors and playing freely in the sunshine and wind, Aneeda could be found in her favorite bloodstone bowling alley. "Come on, sisters, let's go bowling! I love how the rolling balls sound like thunder and my strikes crack like lightening!"

"Aneeda, you're amazing! You are such a solid sister, and you make us feel connected to all life, especially to your nature family of animals, plants, creepy crawlies, and even the weather!"

"That's my job, girls. I *need* that connection. I was born to be a strong foundation for all of us. I will gladly protect and maintain my position here on the ground floor!" Giving a sharp little salute with pride, she continued, "I thrive when I am connected to you . . .

and to our crystal castle . . . and to the entire community of Thisis-meville . . . and to the whole world! I just need to have a roof over my head, healthy food to eat, adequate exercise, and a family who loves me. That's not too much to ask, is it?"

"Aneedahavemyneedsmet. Aneedagoodhome. Aneeda-placetoexercise. Aneedalotofhealthyfood. Aneedaknowibelong. Aneedaknowi'msafe. Aneedabeabundant!"

"We are your sister tribe, Aneeda. We trust your support for us. We need you too, so we can be our healthiest! You can always count on us to gladly receive all the strong, stable, and sturdy energy you have to give," said her six sisters in unison.

Aneeda often reflected on how loved she felt, and in turn, how much she loved everybody else. She had a strong trust and belief in the goodness of life. All of her basic necessities were fulfilled with ease when she remembered her worthiness to receive the abundance around her in all its many forms. Life was good and healthy on Mt. Iknowmenow when Aneeda's needs were met.

5

2nd Floor, Ivanna:
The Sensual Sister—
I Want

Every morning, the sisters would climb the golden spiral staircase to visit each other. They embraced one another with appreciation and happiness, and chatted about the color and energy vibrations that made intricate patterns on their individual floors.

The abundance of space inside the crystal castle felt as infinite as the whole cosmos. Each floor was unique and limitless, like creation itself. Ivanna's creativity and enthusiasm was as large as her entire floor. Although Ivanna's consciousness did not spin as fast as the sisters on the floors above her, her speed suited her desires just fine.

Ivanna lived between the vibrant reds on Aneeda's floor and the bright sunshine yellow in Ahafta's home above. Her sisters generously spilled their light upward and downward, creating Ivanna's energizing orange glow on the second floor.

Bright auburn waves bounced freely on Ivanna's head, and her hazel eyes sparkled with passion and enjoyment—especially when she expressed herself through movement. As a young chakra child she filled the castle with her playful requests: "Ivanna play! Ivanna dance! Ivanna laugh! Listen to my jingling bells, sisters! Let's do some belly dancing! Bet you can't swivel your hips like I can!"

As Ivanna grew a little older, her body moved with grace and speed when the tempo called for it, sometimes causing the second floor of the castle to quiver and rock around.

Ivanna flowed with life as she matured, shifting and rearranging things if the castle's energy began to feel a little sluggish from inactivity or a rare lack of movement on any floor. She was very close to her sister Aneeda, whose heavy earth energy slowed things down a little too much for Ivanna's quicker pace. Ivanna's nature was to keep everything moving with graceful fluidity, and it was no problem for her to be the initiator of change for the castle, since a new transformation of any kind was always exciting for this sacral chakra princess. When her friends from Thisismeville spotted the castle's orange lights undulating ever so slightly from the second floor, they knew Ivanna must be shaking a sumptuous shimmy, or exercising her lower back to keep it open and flexible.

A lighthearted, optimistic energy was the norm for the feminine Ivanna, and she was constantly inviting a reason to celebrate everything. Sensuous fabrics of chiffon and silk hung from high wooden beams while sweet fragrances of cinnamon filled the air. Orange marigolds and peach daylilies spilled over in huge bouquets, emitting a warm and cheerful feeling. Ivanna often snuggled up with her favorite calico cat on ginger-colored pillows strewn about her double bed covered with vibrant tangerine throws.

The second floor of the castle was also a water sanctuary, filled with carvings of whales, seals, and eels made of citrine quartz. A small altar in Ivanna's room held golden topaz carvings of her favorite dolphins, sea horses, and starfish. This chakra sister had been a water baby from the first moment her tiny fingers could make little swirls in the warm liquid of her bath. She loved to blow bubbles and squish her toes in the mud after a rainstorm. Waterfalls poured under the spiral staircases from her floor, and their clear, energizing sprays recharged her energy.

"Ivanna, you seem happiest when you are near the water."

"You bet I am. Give me a slow stream, a rushing river, or the wild waves of the ocean any day. You should see the paintings of the surf I just created on the decks of my indoor swimming pools."

"Oh sisters, have you seen Ivanna's latest creation? asked Aneeda, who was proud of Ivanna's artistic talents.

"Is it that huge mirror in her foyer? The one she framed with tiger's-eye, and terra-cotta stones?"

"Do you like it?" asked Ivanna, always eager for approval. "I made it really large . . . all the better to see myself in full view!" This chakra sister knew what she wanted and never hesitated to say it. With help from her sister Singya, Ivanna expressed herself by making up rhythmical tunes about tropical sunsets and singing them into the ponds around Thisismeville.

Birds of paradise

Deep sea treasures

I'm Ivanna

Bring me pleasures!

Like yin and yang, Ivanna had a lot in common with her ground floor sister, Aneeda. Not needing as much, she did, however, *want* almost as much. Ivanna always had a powerful creative urge to merge with something new, and her magnetism easily brought opposites together—man and woman, the sun and the moon, up and down, in and out.

Ivanna's compulsion to taste, touch, smell, see, hear, and enjoy everything life had to offer kept her sisters on their toes. They helped Ivanna discipline her endless desires by reminding her to make a choice and finally land on something, but it was hard to catch this social butterfly who flitted so quickly from one thing to the next.

As Ivanna matured, she was the life of every party she threw and knew just how to be the perfect hostess. It was a challenge for this personality princess to mind her own business since it was her nature to be intimately drawn to others, but her sisters kept Ivanna on their radar to make sure that her sympathy for others and her empathy for how someone else was feeling didn't pull her down. If Ivanna fell into someone else's drama, it affected all the sisters and pulled them out of alignment with each other.

"Ivanna, thank you for being so comfortable in your own skin. You exude a natural sexuality that attracts a lot of friends to us!"

Ivanna purred back like the natural flamboyant actress that she could be, "Ivanna be loved by you!"

"If only we had your long waves of auburn hair that snuggle so perfectly into your cleavage!"

"Girls, jealousy is not helpful to our unified cause!" reminded Iamone, ignoring their giggling. "Remember, our job is to temper Ivanna's moods."

"Yes, but it is my job to let Ivanna know that she has the right to express her emotions however she pleases," said Singya, the expressive sister on the fifth floor.

"Score, Singya!" shouted Ivanna, a little too enthusiastically. "Tempering my moods is not much fun, Ms. Party Pooper, Iamone."

Iamone smiled at her little emotional sister.

"But it drives me crazy when Ivanna whines, 'I want what I want, and I want it now!'" complained Ahafta, ironically, since she was the tenacious sister one floor above.

The chakra sisters remembered times when Ivanna had the impetus to be a little drama princess, which sometimes turned into tantrums and outbursts. They recalled one story in particular and loved bringing it to Ivanna's attention just to see her response. Since there was a never-ending pool of sweetness and sensuality around Ivanna, they could lovingly tease her like sisters usually do, knowing that no one took any ribbing too seriously.

"Ivanna, remember the time you threw that wild get-together?"

"When you found whatshername . . . some girl you knew . . . who was outrageously flirting with your escort?"

"Oh, don't remind me," laughed Ivanna. "That was long ago."

"You certainly were not very charming that evening."

"I remember it well," said Useeme, who knew every move and thought each sister made.

"Oooo," mimicked Singya, pretending to be Ivanna getting ready for her party, "feel these fabrics. Such rich textures! Girls, I'm having a little intimate gathering tonight. Look what I'll be wearing. . . . Do you like this new silk robe? It's hand-painted in my favorite shades of copper and rust."

They reminisced about that night long ago, reenacting their animated conversations.

"Uh oh, Ivanna's indulging herself in luxury again!" teased Ahafta, who was not nearly as frivolous as her sister on the second floor. "I thought I was hot, but you take the cake, sister!"

"Ivanna, you always bring beauty into our castle. Look at your fancy dangly earrings made of citrine crystals!"

"All the better to have my suitors nibble there a bit before moving into a closer embrace!" Her sisters chuckled at Ivanna's one-track mind and how she was so naturally theatrical about it.

"And multiple bracelets of carnelian and moonstones. Mm-hmmm . . . you are one sexy sacral chakra sister," whistled Singya, just to enliven the compliments that Ivanna was soaking up.

Ahluvya, who teased less than her sisters, added, "Ivanna, I do love your new silk robe and how it matches your hair!"

"And this long amber bead necklace is beautiful, too!" added Iamone, although she was the sister of higher thoughts and really had no interest in material things like jewelry or clothes.

The seven chakra sisters accepted and supported each other with unconditional love for just who they were. Their relationship with one another worked in harmony because they were wise enough to never get offended or take things too personally.

"And wasn't it just so delicious when I served my favorite fleshy sweet potatoes and luscious mangoes?" said Ivanna, as she glossed and then smacked her full lips together. "I'm glad our friends stuck around for dessert. It was so satisfying when everyone shared slices of succulent oranges and slurped on some slippery peaches!"

"Yes, good thing you still had friends by the end of the evening, because the disaster happened before dessert!"

"That's an understatement!" said Useeme. "I saw your jealous green eyes that night, Ivanna."

"You had the nerve to sashay over to them and 'accidentally' trip on the corner of your exotic oriental carpet."

"It was a horrible scene, I know," admitted Ivanna. "I forgot my manners."

"You forgot your divine perfection!" reminded Iamone.

"I can't believe you spilled our favorite—"

"—and *expensive*—" (The sisters were used to filling in each other's sentences.)

"—imported red wine all over your guest's pretty white party dress. What a mess!"

"Not only a mess, but what a waste of a perfectly good bottle!" added Aneeda, the practical sister who appreciated the basic needs of nourishment and valued every last drop of drink or morsel of food.

"Alright, so I wasn't exactly being nice to her."

"Another understatement," repeated Useeme.

"Owl Woman warned you about your tendencies to overstep your boundaries because of jealousy, Ivanna, and you have to take responsibility for all of your desires and choices, for our sake."

"I know. I know! It was times like that when I really hated having the gift of clairsentience. I could feel just how she was feeling at that moment. Ouch. Pretty embarrassing for me, too."

"Good thing you remembered yourself and finally apologized to her. That made all of us feel so much better!" said Ahluvya, who also couldn't stand to see or feel when anyone was hurt.

"She was a flirt that night, just like I can be sometimes," admitted Ivanna. "Fortunately, she turned out to be a good sport about everything after all. Sorry, sisters, and thanks for putting up with my unpredictable moods."

Six chakra sisters crowded around the emotional one and gave her a group hug. "It's all good, Ivanna, you know we love you like a big taffy apple . . . sweet and sticky!"

"Speak for yourselves, girls," said Aneeda, "but you know I would prefer a simple organic red potato to keep us grounded."

"Say what you will, sisters," quipped Ivanna, "but you know that I keep life juicy here on the second floor of our castle. Without me, we'd be all dried up and way too boring!"

"Touché!"

When Ivanna wanted and received whatever pleasures made her happy, the entire castle on Mt. Iknowmenow was happy.

6

3rd Floor, Ahafta:
The Motivated Sister—
I Have To

Even though the chakra sisters were septuplets, each one considered her sisters on the floors above as an older sibling. As they climbed the staircase, they could feel the energy change. Each floor had a slightly more mature sense than the previous one, as if they somehow had a little more advanced experience or wisdom. Ahafta kept the third floor of the castle in excellent condition, which made her proud of herself and gave her the idea to call her siblings "little."

As little children, when the chakra sisters would visit Ahafta's room, they chased each other around giant urns of yellow sunflowers, barely missing the lemon-scented candles that lit up the third floor.

"Be careful, girls. Don't crash into my solar panels!" pleaded the third floor sister. "You know I thrive on the sun's fire which gives me the energy I need to stay motivated and focused."

Remembering her charge from Owl Woman, Ahafta knew that she would have to use all the powerful fire energy that burned on this floor wisely. Ahafta was diligent about keeping the passionate flames of her personal power in check. Her body burned with determination to be the best achiever in the castle. "Tame my flame. Tame my flame," was the mantra that reminded Ahafta of her responsibility to empower herself and others without overwhelming them.

On the ground floor, Aneeda needed her family and the entire town of Thisismeville around her so she could feel like she belonged to a large group of people. Ivanna on the second floor wanted more specific one-on-one relationships. But Ahafta held a different vibration on the third floor; she had to have the freedom to be herself, and unlike her sisters below her, Ahafta had a fierce determination to be her own independent boss.

"Aneeda and Ivanna's energy pull downward naturally, like gravity and water, where they feel most comfortable. But I know how much energetic work it takes to bring my two little sisters up to my floor for the journey toward higher consciousness. My challenge is to find a bulldozer, or a magnet, or a crane large enough to hoist their big, heavy—"

"Ahafta!" interrupted Singya, who was always listening from up on the fifth floor. "I can hear what you almost said about your little sisters!"

"Oops," was all Ahafta could say.

"It's not like we live in one tiny room together, we're in a huge castle! But we're still close enough that nothing anyone says or does is hidden from any of us. There's plenty of space for everyone to grow here, even with our differences, but we must always respect one another," reminded Ahluvya.

"Oh, right. . . . I know that," answered Ahafta, who just wanted to get on with her own business.

The third floor housed the castle's engine that got the life force moving upward, so ignition and combustion were Ahafta's specialties. Born with the Fire element, Ahafta was literally the hottest sister of all the chakra princesses in the castle. She tossed a voluminous mane of golden blonde hair over her shoulder. Her dark eyes pierced the world around her, and her air of confidence spilled over into others, making them believe in themselves, too. Sometimes Ahafta's inner feelings pushed her engines into overdrive, and then she would call out to her sister below, "Ivanna, I'm overheated and I need to de-stress! I'm coming downstairs to take a quick dip in your cooling pools!"

Ahafta also recharged her batteries in her third floor yoga studio, where a fire pit blazed in the center of the room. The roaring fire was background music to Ahafta. She, like Ivanna, loved to be on the move and would often break into a spontaneous dance to the sound of the crackling flames.

"I am strong! I am brave! I am powerful! I can do anything!" she would recite, while gazing into her own willful eyes in the mirror.

Observing Ahafta practice her daily meditative fire breathing, Useeme commented, "Ahafta, you're panting like a dog!"

"Look at your belly. How do you make it roll in and out like that?"

"Try it! My breath of fire will be stronger than yours, but keep trying . . . it will give you big muscles in your tummies, clear your mind, and make you be superwomen!" said Ahafta, eager to empower her sisters. "It's easy. Just pull your stomach in real fast on every exhale—but do it quickly to make your energy move! Don't force it, be gentle. This takes practice. That's it. Now try it through your nose. It just takes a minute to do."

Over time, Useeme appreciated Ahafta's breathing exercises because it increased the flow of oxygen to her brain, which made every chakra princess feel rejuvenated and revitalized.

"Come on, sisters, let's race up the golden staircase!" Ahafta was always ready to climb to the top, knowing she could easily win any challenge that she might face. Leading the way, up and up, encouraging her sisters, Ahafta emphasized her personal chant more with each step.

Feel my fire

of desire

to inspire.

Let's go higher!

"Hey, I'm the one who has all the desires in this castle, not Ahafta!" teased Ivanna, reminding her sisters how much she loved their attention.

As confident as Ahafta was, she was also wise enough to know that she still needed the guidance of her four sisters on the upper floors and the emotional stability of her two sisters below her.

"Useeme, you are the visionary in the castle. Please help me understand this crazy dream I had last night."

"What did you eat before you went to sleep?" asked Aneeda, again showing her natural concern for healthy food and how her sisters were nourishing themselves. "That might indicate how you've been following your gut instincts . . . or not."

"I had my favorite snack of yellow peas, golden peppers, and tart pineapples, and then I stretched out on my tan leather couch. When I fell asleep, I saw huge yellow canaries wearing half-cut lemon helmets. They were sword fighting with overripe bananas!"

"Well, it's not off the charts, considering how fearless you are about taking risks, Ahafta, but I think there is a deep message in this dream about your strong sense of inner value and personal worth," said Singya, the sister of intuitive listening.

"Really?" asked Ahafta. "What would wild canaries and bananas have to do with my natural assertiveness and high self-esteem?"

"I love your humility, Ahafta; it's so dignified!" joked Aneeda.

Useeme was the best at interpreting dreams and answered, "Sword fighting is normal for your competitive nature, Ahafta. And since you always *have* to achieve, you must be upset with yourself for procrastinating about something, which is why your fruit is about to spoil."

"Oh, interesting!" said Ivanna in her usual sensual way. "I wasn't thinking *that* about those bananas at all!"

Ahafta rolled her eyes and was grateful to have the input of her four "older" and more mature sisters to guide her.

"Those helmets are telling you to not let too many bitter lemons in life sour your thinking."

"I can get a little too obsessive about work, can't I?" admitted Ahafta with sincere honesty. "Thanks for the reminder, girls. But what's with the giant canaries?"

"Ahafta," said Useeme as kindly as she could, "I think they are reminding you to let yourself fly free and stop competing with yourself so much. Remember to sing and allow yourself to play a little more!"

"I can help you do that, gladly!" laughed Ahluvya.

"You are definitely our most motivated sister, Ahafta, with an attitude that fits your name . . . Ahaftahavethis. Ahaftadothat. Ahaftaprovemyselftome. Ahaftaccomplishagoal. Ahaftabemotivated. Ahaftatakearisk. Ahaftahavepower. Ahaftagetitdone!"

"Thanks, sisters. You do offer wise counsel indeed!"

"I agree," said Singya, "and I love Useeme's advice about remembering to sing!"

"Life is really all about our attitudes and how we think about things, isn't it? My accomplishments don't mean anything if I am hurting any one of you, so I will remember to lighten up for your sake," said Ahafta.

"Well, that's certainly good news, since all work and no play makes us all a bit grumpy!"

"We are all one. Remember that, sisters!" exclaimed Iamone, the wisest chakra princess with spiritual knowing. "Your message is a message for the whole castle, Ahafta. When you succeed, we succeed. When you are confident, we all feel high self-esteem. When you are thinking positively and you are you, Ahafta, we are unstoppable! Just don't forget to keep things in their proper perspective. Your achievements only have true value when they are made with our highest purpose in mind—and, of course, consideration for how every decision you make affects others."

"We depend on you to help us get things done in the castle, Ahafta."

"Aneeda is right," said Ivanna. "Without your motivation I don't know how we would accomplish anything."

When Ahafta fired up her determination, she was empowered. When she felt empowered, all the sisters were courageous and thought highly of themselves. When Ahafta stoked her flames, the whole castle was motivated to grow, flow, and glow.

7

4th Floor, Ahluvya:
The Loving Sister—
I Love

"Come upstairs and be in love with me!" says the sister of the heart, opening her arms wide, her emerald green eyes sparkling. Ahluvya's floor felt different from any other in the crystal castle. Unlike the solid earthiness of Aneeda's ground floor, or the watery nature of Ivanna, or Ahafta's fire energy, the fourth floor was open and spacious, with fresh, flowing breezes.

Multiple pink quartz mobiles hung in the expansive hallway, which gave this chakra sister's space a calm yet floating sensation to all who entered her floor. Knowing that her massive heart space could make people feel a bit woozy, Ahluvya learned to be kind and compassionate toward everyone and worked to help bring them back into balance when this happened. Her ability to balance the physical body with the spiritual realm created a comfortable place to relax into the awareness of such powerful love.

Fragrances of ylang ylang and geraniums perfumed the fourth floor, and fresh pink rose petals blew in intricate patterns wherever Ahluvya walked. The heart chakra sister's graceful steps were like delicate dandelions blowing in the wind, spreading soft, tiny seeds of inspiration around her. Everyone felt connected to her inner beauty as well as her outer beauty. As a true crystal castle child, Ahluvya's divine energy held the frequencies of pink innocence and fun, like strawberry bubblegum ice cream.

Enormous heart-shaped malachite carvings stood like angelic sentinels, accenting her interior hallways. Green lotuses filled her oversize diamond and peridot bathtub while pink orchids and stargazer lilies overflowed from large aquamarine urns. Ahluvya had the ability to take flight in her loving heart and mind, and her walls mirrored this skill with jade- and fuchsia-colored feathers that gently flapped in the wind from a multitude of ornamental fans. Like the breathing lungs of the castle, these oscillating fans caused a collection of crystal and glass wind chimes to constantly clink soft, soothing sounds.

As Owl Woman promised, Ahluvya would be the great balancer in the castle. Her spiritual gift of balancing came in handy whenever Aneeda got lazy, or Ivanna partied too hard, or the high-powered Ahafta got too hot, or the cacophony of sounds, voices, and opinions coming from expressive Singya became too strong. Ahluvya's meditations allowed her to center herself in her own stillness, enveloping herself in a comforting quilt of green healing light, always bringing her sisters back into alignment with peace.

Ahluvya was not only the heart sister; she also carried the living air and breath of the castle. Mindful breathing was Ahluvya's spiritual practice. Green and pink were her colors, and her element of air blew these colorful vibrations through the middle of the castle and then upward and downward, touching all of her sisters on their own floors.

"Ahhh, breathe," sighed Ahluvya, inhaling a deep breath of Ahafta's warm yellow light from the floor below her. "I'll mix that with another big whiff of Singya's cool blue light from one flight above and create my favorite soothing green energy."

"Ahluvya, your green light is a magical healing tonic for our castle," said her sisters. "The power of your love keeps us balanced between our daily work in the world and our joy of simply being. You remind us to be in love with every breath you take!"

"It's always my pleasure to remind you of the power of love, sisters. It heals everything. When life gets too hectic and you feel like you've lost your way, just breathe into my heart where I will soothe all of your stress. Then the castle can be at peace again."

Never passing up the opportunity to be heard, Ahafta and Singya both boasted, "We're all in this together, sisters. Don't forget that it is our yellow and blue lights that give Ahluvya her green heart power!"

"And what about me?" asked Aneeda. "It is my red vibration that gives the pink glow to this floor . . . that is, when Iamone shares her white light all the way down to me on the ground, right?"

"Of course," agreed Ahluvya. "We all need each other's specific frequency if we want to blend into more creative expressions. Owl Woman taught us that the whole is greater than its parts. Remember that . . . and take a breath!"

The fourth floor was the most expansive and airy space in the castle, and Ahluvya loved her bedroom, being in the very center of the central floor of the castle, the most. She felt at peace with herself and her surroundings there. Shining emeralds emblazoned her ceiling, and bright green foliage hung from the rafters and over the doors. Pink and green ivy vines draped in and around her leafy patterned furniture, and large ferns curled like lovable pets over her pillows and four-poster bed.

Ahluvya understood her root-bound sister Aneeda because they both needed nature to nourish them well. But while Aneeda preferred to be alone with Mother Earth, Ahluvya wanted to connect with the whole world as if she was Mother Earth herself, holding and nurturing everyone. On the fourth floor everything that grows green was alive and thriving in every corner. Ahluvya walked barefoot over thick grasses that grew inside like lush carpets over her wooden floors. Soft peat moss provided a curving walkway throughout the fourth floor that led to a verdant forest and her private greenhouse. There, Ahluvya tended to her pink rose bushes, lime trees, kiwi vines, and endless rows of broccoli, asparagus, green beans, leafy lettuces, spinach, and peas. Of all these staples of Ahluvya's healthy food choices, she also made sure she juiced her daily green servings of fresh, energizing wheatgrass.

Ahluvya's heart was a large enough place for everything, and she easily accepted it all just as it was, without any preconceived conditions or judgments. The chakra princess on the fourth floor had such a blissful countenance nothing could stop her willingness to share her heart with others. Feeling centered in her vast open space of love and optimism, Ahluvya was connected to everyone and everything around her, especially her six chakra sisters. She sang out to Singya, Useeme, and Iamone, "You are my spiritual sugars!" And to the sisters on the three floors below her, Ahluvya would sing, "You are my earthy spices!" Then, spreading her arms wide, she chanted joyfully to all, "I love us seven sisters, because we're everything that nice is!" Loving others blessed Ahluvya with a sense of purpose, which gave her even more reason to love herself. She had no expectations about how anyone else should be; she just loved for the sake of loving.

Often, Ahluvya would shout gleefully outside, up toward the heavens in gratitude and awe for life. Even sweeter notes poured out when she used her serene heart and breath to play her handmade rosewood flute. When she prayed and played like a master piper, the air felt as light as a baby's kiss and flowed in a steady current around the castle, drawing people inward toward Ahluvya's mesmerizing notes.

One bright morning, a mystical bird heard her magical flute playing and came to Ahluvya's window. It had beautiful jade, blue-green, aqua, and purple iridescent feathers that shimmered and sparkled in the sunlight like a giant dragonfly. Its birdsong was crisp and high, "MeeWee! MeeWee! MeeWee!" The strange bird kept calling until Ahluvya gave it her full attention. The sound reminded her of an ancient memory . . . but what? MeeWee . . . Where had she heard that before?

The MeeWee bird continued to call after that, and its essence remained on the open windowsill until years later when Ahluvya would finally understand the mysterious creature's profound spiritual message.

When Ahluvya's heart was open, all the sisters in the castle felt snuggled in a cocoon of unconditional love.

8

5th Floor, Singya:
The Expressive Sister—
I Tell It Like It Is

The fifth floor of the magical crystal castle, designed as a cool blue circular space, housed Singya and her infinite sound waves. The atmosphere on Singya's floor was even lighter than Ahluvya's. The unique rounded architecture reflected her skillful art of communicating in complete form, making sense from beginning to end, like a circle. Singya was continuously expressing herself, whether it was through speaking, singing, playing a musical instrument, writing or listening. Even her thick hair rippled in expressive waves, highlighted with the hues of the blues.

Singya's throat chakra sounds and vibrations reverberated through the small azure studio space in ripples of specific resonance. She was aware that her vibrations could bring either harmony or dis-chord into the castle. It was Ahluvya's love coming up from the floor beneath that allowed Singya to be the most effective spokesperson for all of her sisters, creating a pleasant hum of harmonious rhythms between them and the world outside of the crystal castle. When Aneeda needed something, Singya helped her articulate her request. When Ivanna wanted something, Singya encouraged her to express her desires with clarity. Ahafta spoke with confidence because Singya kept her honest and gave her just the right words to say at the right time. Singya was proud of her ability to choose her precise words concisely to get the sisters' point across. "Speak up and speak out, sisters! It's the only way to know if you are being an effective communicator!"

"You mean, if we're not sitting in silence or meditating," said Useeme, "which is my effective way of communicating with spirit."

"Or just being in a loving frame of mind," added Ahluvya. "Did you know that our heart communicates with a stronger frequency than any other part of our castle?"

"OK, sisters, you got me on this one. You are right," Singya acquiesced. "There are many ways to communicate. My job is to keep you honest with yourself and others in whatever way you wish to express yourself."

Owl Woman often visited the castle to surprise her goddess girls with gifts. "My lovely enchantress, Singya, I found these rare turquoise stones in the lands from our ancient indigenous cultures. Look closely and you will see the colors of the red earth and blue sky together. I thought you might decorate your walls with these beauties!" The birdwoman proudly showed off her ability to pick the perfect present for no reason at all, but she knew that in this case the healing properties of turquoise would instinctively remind Singya of her gift of being able to bring two distinct notes together, like the earth with the air, the body with the mind, the heart with spirit.

While Ahluvya bridged the physical life of her sisters' bodies to the higher spiritual realms, it was Singya who opened the gateway to the upper worlds. "I will help you express the most spiritually loving vibrations in everything you create, sisters. I do this best because I live between the heart of Ahluvya and the mind of Useeme."

"Yes, Singya, you are the bridge that links the body with the mind and spirit," said Iamone. "Without you, our little sisters wouldn't be able to bring Useeme's insights or my spiritual wisdom into the world."

Owl Woman gloated, "That's right! Just like these powerful turquoise stones! I knew they'd be perfect for Singya's floor."

The special acoustics on the fifth floor resounded with ethereal qualities, allowing Singya to more easily reach the mystical realms. She communicated with angels and spirit guides by using ultrasensitive sound waves. Her four chakra sisters on the floors below her could not "hear" the celestial sounds that came easily to Singya, so this chakra princess took pride in integrating these higher-self frequencies into their daily lives.

The bustling energy on the fifth floor had various voices of both high and low pitches chanting, toning, and singing in strange, syncopated rhythms. Like the backstage of a grand symphony, there were pianos a-playing, stringed instruments a-plucking, drums a-drumming, six geese a-laying, and five golden rings a-singing in Singya's cozy living space. This was always a pleasant cacophony for those who entered the fifth floor, and the many sounds that kept Singya's creativity flowing.

Singya could speak multiple languages at a very young age. She learned how to work with guttural sounds from her throat, squeezing her lips in just the right way to create the proper accentuations. It was Singya who taught Aneeda how to adeptly roll her r's.

Urging her sisters to play with her, Singya spoke of the funny feelings inside her head when she made her special sounds. "Come on, sisters . . . pucker your lips like this. Then puff out your cheeks and stretch your mouth wide. That's it! Now, flap your tongue in every direction. Let's hear some sound with that!" she cheered.

"*Zzzzzz . . . jjjjjjjrrrrrssssss . . . uullwwooooo . . . aaahhhhh . . . oooohhhmmmmm.* Hold the *m. Hooold* the *mmmmmm!* It will wake you up and make your teeth squeak! Come on, try it!"

"You're weird, Singya . . . but a lot of fun."

"Now make sure the corners of your lips reach all the way up to your ears. Let me see those cheek muscles flex! This is how we warm up our face before we send our words out into the world." Singya had a way of keeping all her sisters smiling.

While there was usually some kind of music playing from singing bowls humming or tuning forks clinking any time day or night, Singya also reveled in her sacred times of pure silence too, when even her favorite bluebirds fell mute for her benefit. Singya could be found every morning on her round sky-blue meditation pillow quietly sitting in tranquil silence, listening deep inside her head, as if she was falling through long tunnels within her ears that swirled into the center of her brain. These were the moments when Singya's active mind slowed down and her quieted thoughts could then create the most valuable and meaningful words to communicate outwardly.

"*Shhhh* . . . I'm listening," demanded Singya. "Can't you hear the angels whispering? I can hear the celestial chorus! Listen!" In her stillness and deeper listening, Singya was always nourished by hearing the divine voice within. "Sisters, we're getting an important message from a master teacher!"

"What? What's it saying?" asked Aneeda. "I need to hear everything!"

"No, tell *me!*" begged Ivanna. "I want to hear the message from the teacher!"

"I have to hear it first!" demanded Ahafta. "I *have* to, or I'll burst!"

"I would love for you to share it with me, Singya," purred light-hearted Ahluvya.

Singya relished her clairaudient skills. "The message is . . ."

"What?! What *is* it?" shouted the chakra sisters from the four floors below Singya.

"The message is . . ." Singya had their attention and played out her game ever so slowly, "I hear it now. Clearly . . ."

"What?! Stop teasing, Singya!" groaned Ivanna.

"OK. Listen closely now. The message from our angelic master teacher is saying, 'Be good sisters and bring a big bowl of plump blueberries up to the fifth floor for a lip-smackin' superfood party!"

Aneeda, Ivanna, Ahafta, and Ahluvya screamed in delight, realizing they'd fallen once again for another practical joke from their good-natured sister on the fifth floor. They had plenty of practice chasing after Singya for her endless teasing, albeit kindhearted and innocent, and they knew how to run up the spiral staircase faster than lightning.

"We could choke you when your sense of humor stings us, Singya," said her sisters, "so thank Goddess that Ahluvya's heart light keeps hurt and sarcasm out of your voice!"

It was true. Ahluvya kept her soft, loving green heart energy pointed directly into Singya's blue throat so that she would always speak with gentleness and focused spiritual willpower, never judgment, exaggeration, or gossip.

Singya trusted and listened to her own inner voice, which was audible to her at all times. This kicked up her intuitive senses and enhanced her art of listening to others as well, though most of what she heard was not actually being said aloud.

Since her living quarters were smaller than her sisters, this bouncy child kept her room clean and uncluttered. Other than the mountains of blueberries that she snacked upon daily, Singya lived in the purest environment possible to better distill the large amounts of information received by her antennae for the castle's many activities. As she listened deeply, she assimilated her sisters' many thoughts and then integrated them into a coherent whole. Communication was the key to Singya speaking with integrity for the entire castle. She made the final decisions about exactly what was spoken and how it was phrased. "I mean what I say and I say what I mean," professed the fifth floor chakra sister with the brilliant turquoise eyes.

Singya took her job seriously, but she always made time for singing in wild happiness the song her godmother had given her at birth:

I am free.

I am free.

I am free to be me!

This little chant helped all of Singya's sisters feel free to be themselves too.

Singya understood how language could empower or intimidate her sisters, so she stressed sincere and articulate speech with delicate craftsmanship. Her sisters would often ask Singya, "What should we express today? What shade of azure should we wear, Singya? How should we style our hair? Which shoes do you like best with this outfit?" or "Am I being truly heard today?" These questions made Singya laugh heartily, for she knew that no matter how they wanted to express themselves, they would find their own answers for their collective choice, with Singya's energy being their guiding voice.

"Just get out there and be yourself!" sang Singya. "Sing your own songs in harmony and honesty with one another. Create your life using all of your talents and abilities. Express clearly what you are thinking and how you are feeling. Not everyone around you will be a mind reader, you know!"

Now this chakra sister was beginning to sound a little like their beloved godmother, Owl Woman. "Remember sisters, to be truly free, you must always express your truth!"

When Singya sang her truest heart song, the whole castle stood strong in its authentic spiritual expression.

9

6th Floor, Useeme:
The Intuitive Sister—
I See Everything

Climbing higher now to the sixth floor of the castle, Useeme's living space was unique, like Singya's, although larger in scope. Useeme was the chakra sister nearest to Iamone on the top floor. They were closely connected to each other, and their brilliant minds were always communicating on the top two floors.

Useeme's floor had the most complex design in the castle. Electromagnetic energy flowed through wires arranged to fit perfectly into Useeme's brain life pattern. Her intricate networks spanned between the hills and valleys on Mt. Iknowmenow so she could keep in contact with the community. When the wisdom of nature grew the chakra sisters' crystal castle, a unique mainframe was imbedded on the sixth floor, just for Useeme. Yes, even an ancient crystal castle had its control panels.

"What do you think, Iamone—shall we hover for a while and observe our sisters? We can bring their subconscious thoughts up to a higher conscious awareness."

"Useeme," replied her big sister, "you really need to relax a little more! I trust that our sisters are doing just fine learning about life in their own way. Try not to hover so much. Just give them the freedom to explore the world. Remember, our sisters' mistakes might be their greatest opportunities to learn. Besides, we are already enlightened, remember? Earth life is our playground where we can allow joy to flourish."

Useeme knew that Iamone was purely loving with her advice, but she didn't feel comfortable simply surrendering her ultimate responsibility. Useeme's purpose was to run the main computer system in the castle. She was the top operator of all the wiring which connected the minds of all her chakra sisters. Constantly on watch, she was the command and control princess who kept vigil on her sisters below her. Useeme had an uncanny ability to catch the slightest variation of thoughts in the system; she would see warning lights and reroute the signals before they could manifest any danger within the castle. She was in charge of all thought forms created by her sisters, but she knew it was not her place to judge them as good or bad—even with Iamone's energy and spiritual inspiration to guide her. Together, Useeme and Iamone raised the vibrations of their sisters' thoughts so the positive side outweighed any negativity.

"Useeme? Do you see me?"

"I see you, Iamone, and if you can see me, you can be me, for I am Useeme!"

"What do you see in me?" asked her sisters, collectively vying for Useeme's attention. "I see me in you and I see you in me. I am Useeme."

"Uh oh . . . Useeme sees me and we see Useeme!" and on and on it went.

With her wide-angle view, Useeme had the advantage of seeing not just with two physical eyes, but with an inner third eye as well. This chakra sister could see and know everything that was happening on all the floors below her, sometimes causing her little sisters to balk at this talent.

"Stop spying on us, Useeme! We can't get away with anything!"

"That's my plan, girls. Don't forget that I'm always watching you!"

"Creepy, peeping sister," teased Ivanna.

"From the position of the higher mind," explained Ahluvya, "both Useeme and Iamone seem to float in a different type of spiritual realm without the physical world of sensations, feelings, and emotions that hold our attention."

"Very astute of you to notice, Ahluvya!" acknowledged Useeme.

"What makes you so unique, Useeme, is your calm, cool, and collected personality, which matches all *three* of your dark blue all-seeing eyes!"

Useeme laughed and tossed her head back, and her sisters were amazed that her cropped hair didn't move at all. It shined like a blue-black pearl. A single indigo curl in the shape of a swirl rested on the center of her forehead, framing her delicate third eye.

Because her third eye was actively open, Useeme excelled in the psychic arts. She often had visions of angels and mystical beings from other times and dimensions, and she hung out with enlightened spiritual allies. Her gifts of clairvoyance and prophetic dreams gave Useeme the ability to see what was happening not only in Thisismeville but also in the world far beyond. Although she knew it was her responsibility to share her inner wisdom with her sisters, she also knew the importance of setting boundaries to keep too many outside or intrusive psychic occurrences from overwhelming or confusing her.

"Girls, be aware of the media! Sometimes the things I see are full of propaganda and will try to make you believe you are less than who you truly are. Don't fall for illusions! Be smart. What you see is not necessarily real. Does the world see through eyes of conflict or peace? Growth or oppression? Are decisions made that are beneficial and respectful to the earth and all her inhabitants? Only believe that which speaks from the heart of wisdom and love. You'll know it when you hear it—right, Singya? You can easily see it from my viewpoint up here on the sixth floor."

To keep herself on track with her responsibility for the castle, she chanted a personal mantra to assist in her discretion.

I yearn

To learn

The power

To discern!

Useeme taught, invented, inspired, and guided her sisters in many ways. She was happiest when she was giving them new ways to think and explore the depths of the mind. "Meet me in the library of my left wing, sisters, where our brilliant intellectual minds can flourish! The information is endless there. We can learn about anything—architecture, sciences, chemistry, engineering; how to build a time machine, how to fly a helicopter, how to speak an exotic foreign language!"

The right wing of Useeme's floor was the hall of metaphysical knowledge. "Sisters," invites Useeme when she is feeling creative, "let's ignite our imaginations with light. It's my element. Light is the energy of universal information, so we can *think* something and it will manifest!

"We could also paint mandalas in my art studio. Did you know that *mandala* comes from an ancient language called Sanskrit, and it means 'circle'? We can create our own individual designs within the larger structure of the mandala—just like us, being unique parts of the whole castle!"

The girls were always excited to let their spontaneity soar on the right wing of the sixth floor. "We know that this circular process never ends, but for this moment we know that whatever we create with Useeme will be powerful and insightful!"

"And beautiful!" The seven chakra sisters loved and appreciated themselves without question.

Useeme's sisters were in awe of her ability to transform one thing or thought into another. They lovingly called her an alchemist, a mad scientist of the mind, a computer geek who brought amazing dreams from her imagination to fruition for everyone to enjoy. But they each knew that they had their own jobs to do to let that happen, so cooperation was a key component for Useeme's commands to bring a happy life to the castle on Mt. Iknowmenow.

Smack dab in the middle of the sixth floor, connecting the left wing of Useeme's rational, intellectual capabilities with the right wing of her intuitive and psychic abilities, was the sacred inner Insight Chamber, where there was perfect balance. Amethyst geodes and azurite crystals covered the deep indigo-colored walls and low ceiling of this sacred space. Although Useeme surrounded herself with the full spectrum of colors, in this subdued Insight Chamber pure light was refracted, reflected, and projected onto and into endless visual designs, fantasies, and images. In this room, Useeme's dream visions spontaneously shifted into Technicolor scenes with an aurora borealis effect. In the center of the room a kaleidoscope of infinite patterns energized a mysterious pinecone-shaped Flower of Insight held inside a delicate lapis lazuli vase.

During meditation, while Useeme was in a transcendent state of being, a single drop of sweet nectar from the Flower of Insight slowly dripped out the bottom of the vase. The lone drop always landed on Useeme's forehead, and penetrated her brain right behind her physical eyes in the center of her brow. The sacred secretion gave Useeme the ultimate illumination of consciousness, which was how this sister could see all possibilities and probabilities of life. The energetic connection at this precise juncture of prayer, meditation, and insight activated Useeme's powerful intuition, making a dramatic vibration in the whole castle, where all the sisters could see what Useeme sees.

Deep within the Insight Chamber, Useeme practiced quieting her thoughts. In this dark and centered place, she stopped analyzing everything and watched her mind become still and focused. From this state of light, knowing, and love, innovative impulses were downloaded for the castle's greatest welfare. This was where Useeme transmitted the essence of soul to her chakra siblings.

Useeme's spiritual gift was her ability to command her perception to change if it did not resonate with positive energy that would help her and her sisters grow into a full and happy life.

Every day, Useeme said a special command that echoed down the golden spiral staircases and danced like fireflies on her sisters' foreheads, awakening them to a new day. "Discipline our thoughts. . . . Discipline our thoughts!"

"Discipline, sisters, Discipline! We create what we think. I am not in control of you, but I remind you to keep your minds disciplined! We must have mastery of our thoughts at all times! That's the only way we can be free to envision living our lives in harmony together."

Singya smiled whenever she heard this, remembering that Useeme had taught her how to truthfully say exactly what she meant and to mean what she said. Discipline intensified Ahluvya's passion as she felt Useeme's loving commands and kept her thoughts on inclusiveness, not separation. Ahafta knew what Useeme was talking about and disciplined her mind's firepower to get things done on all the practical levels so their collective vision of living in health and happiness could manifest. Ivanna stirred the energy with strong emotions, feeling the excitement for all of her sisters, while Aneeda used her grounding tools to bring Useeme's visions into the physical world of reality.

The castle floors shimmered in their various colors and vibrated with active life when all the chakra sisters were coordinated and working together like this.

Useeme offered encouragement and hope not only to her sisters but also to everyone in Thisismeville to be awake, aware, and alive. "I will remind you that our lives can reach beyond any mundane present circumstances. I will help us see everything from a higher perspective, so we can live in our perfect state of being right now. Imagine evolving into a future with ever-renewing possibilities!"

When Useeme's mastery of her inner visions lit up the castle's imaginative mind, the sisters clearly saw their creative life's purpose.

10
7th Floor, Iamone:
The Spiritual Sister—
I Am One

Iamone lived at the pinnacle of the crystal castle. She was the fairest chakra sister, with bright, almost colorless eyes. Her long white hair flowed in waves down her back, and it always appeared to be blowing from an invisible, far-off breeze. There were times of the year when Iamone shaved her head completely as a devoted act of absolute nonattachment to the material world.

There was a translucent quality to Iamone's skin, which allowed her sisters to see a grid of sparkling golden light within her body and mind. On top of her head, with or without hair, this seventh floor princess sometimes sported a purple crown bejeweled with diamonds, amethysts, and sugilite gemstones.

The seventh floor was not like any other floor in the castle. The walls were transparent and the skylight was always open. The temperature on Iamone's floor remained comfortable because there was no weather at all at this altitude. An iridescent white light illuminated the entire floor, whether it was day or night.

Unlike Aneeda's grounding energy on the first floor, the seventh level defied gravity. Useeme and Iamone worked closely with the elements of Light and Thought, the lightest energies in the crystal castle. Iamone created a buoyant quality in her living space. Her feet gracefully swept along, barely touching the floor.

Iamone was the most serene chakra sister of the septuplets and preferred a Zen-like style to her surroundings. On her altar, a few candles floated in crystal bowls filled with clear glass pebbles. Delicate white lace covered her foodless table, as Iamone fasted most of the time. Oils of frankincense or rose were diffused on the whole floor, unless she was in the mood for a more pungent Indian sandalwood incense. Often, just to satisfy her appreciation of sacred ceremonies, Iamone smudged her floor with white sage, letting the cleansing smoke escape through the roof.

In the center of her room was an elevated, floating bed, which she had to climb into using a very tall stepladder. Her bed's quilt was handmade with gold threads and purple braiding in the shape of a lotus blossom with a thousand unfolding petals. Her pillows were soft, fluffy clouds, carried in by a thousand white butterflies every evening. Velvety violets filled a thousand tiny glass vases that encircled Iamone on her high perch.

Iamone's presence was gentle and quiet compared to her sisters. Her force field was strong and expansive, like Ahluvya's, who accepted all things inside her heart. Iamone, however, knew that she was the field itself. Her connection with the grand universe nourished Iamone. She knew the spiritual science of pure joy and happiness, and for her there was no illusion of separation from anything.

Sometimes Iamone's sisters would quietly sneak up to her room, listening for a new daily mantra. Iamone often chanted softly to herself, and it made her chakra sisters feel blissfully lightheaded.

> *My purpose is our peace, you see . . .*
> *My consciousness is unity.*

To be with one, I simply be.

The Source of All is One in me.

The transcendent feeling in these moments caused the others to practically swoon as they called her name, which sounded like "I-ah-moan" but meant, "I am one." Being one with all was Iamone's pervading essence.

The seventh floor emitted a vast glowing field of wholeness: infinite galaxies, the stars, the planets, the sun and the moon, the earth and her creatures—all of existence was connected through Iamone.

"Good heavens, it gets so crowded up here on the top floor with all this celestial activity!" Even though she saw and knew all there was to know, Iamone still never took herself too seriously.

Everything was unified by Iamone's clear understanding that energy moves and transforms but never disappears. She knew that everything came from one source and at the same time everything *was* the source of all creation. Creation was always being created by creation itself, in Iamone's consciousness.

"Owl Woman was right! I am me and you are me and we are we when we are all together." As Iamone said this she heard a strange etheric chorus faintly in the background, chanting "coo-coo-kachoo, coo-coo-kachoo."

Iamone looked deeply into her memory bank and remembered with inner joy Owl Woman's decree at her naming ceremony: "You are the quintessential radiant chakra sister at the highest level of spiritual and human development, Iamone. You are one with your source of mother-father love. You are one with all of creation! You are *it*, baby, the cat's pajamas!" Once again, Iamone chuckled to herself. In a world of infinite possibilities, she still had never seen a cat wearing pajamas.

Iamone's purpose was to receive and translate divine consciousness from the Queenking in every moment. Since the Queenking was an antenna for the source of all the universal life energy that ran throughout the castle, they needed all their chakra daughters' full cooperation for the wisdom of this life-giving energy to be received and equally distributed throughout all seven floors.

"To get it done . . ." said Ahafta from her third floor,

"We have to love it . . ." said Ahluvya on the fourth floor,

"Into its finest expression!" sang Singya from her circular fifth floor.

Never wanting to be left out, Aneeda from way down on the first floor quickly chimed in, "Yes, but first you need to have my strong foundation to have a step on which to start!"

"And with all of this work, you need me to show you how pleasurable the whole process can be!" said Ivanna, who would never pass up the chance to be noticed, or, better yet, to be the total center of attention.

Useeme and Iamone just shook their heads in amusement as they listened to this collective soliloquy from their sisters below them. "Yes, we know how we must all work together or else the castle might collapse," they laughed lightheartedly, suggesting the idea of the castle actually crumbling as simply preposterous.

"The universal intelligence of this energy is intended for your greatest health and well-being. It brings love, joy, and wisdom into your life experiences, girls, and it is always on your side. Use it wisely—and often!" advised Iamone from her crowning position on the seventh floor.

When Iamone's skylights were open on the seventh floor, all of the sisters connected to Spirit. When they lived from the consciousness of their Higher Self the whole castle felt happy, healthy, loving, and fully engaged with life.

11
Queenking:
The Androgynous
Generator—I Witness

Even higher than Iamone's energy floated the royal penthouse, which hovered above the castle on Mt. Iknowmenow. The Queenking lived here as a reflection of the divine creator of all life throughout the multiverses. The chakra sisters' parental home held the omniscient all-knowing force behind everything that transpired in the castle.

This mother-father love was actually one androgynous self-actualized being, complete with the integrated energies of the divine feminine and the divine masculine. Merging into this oneness made life much easier, leaving them free from having to play the game of the illusion of separation. The enlightened Queenking held the awakened unified force field that gave birth to all things. This field of pure love energized the birth of the seven chakra sisters for the benefit of all. The Queenking consciousness gave the royal mother-father the wisdom to know all things pertaining to the infinite spiritual world and the material earthly realm. They were the main conduit to Iamone's inspiration and sense of oneness.

Because the material plane of the earthly kingdom was one of duality, the compassionate Queenking, though spinning with the same wave and particle frequencies as creation itself, had to become a separate Mother Queen and Father King in order to lower their vibrations enough to enter the castle. It was a rare occasion when the mother-father couple made an actual appearance in the castle, but the princess sisters knew that they were always there for them, constantly beaming unconditional love and spiritual guidance into their little energetic souls. Mostly, the Queenking allowed the chakra sisters to learn life's lessons in their own way and in their own time, rarely interfering with their free will as they matured.

12
The Fundalini's Visit

Iamone's constant union with ultimate Queenking reality granted the seventh floor the most mystical energy of any place in the crystal castle. She knew that it was her job to bring the Queenking's awareness down the castle stairs so that all of her sisters could grow and evolve in this knowing. But the only way Iamone could be authentically herself and help her younger sisters transcend was to invite them up to her level first.

Aneeda, Ivanna, Ahafta, Ahluvya, Singya, and Useeme gave Iamone the nourishment, enthusiasm, movement, love, creative expression, and clear vision needed to take in the vibrations coming through the open skylights of the seventh floor. From atop her lotus bed of being, Iamone's antennae received magnificent messages from the Queenking's spiritual consciousness which must be brought into the world, and her sisters were the ones who had the little legs to make the messages run on the ground.

Aneeda was the anchor of the castle and nothing could be built without her strong foundation supporting everyone else. Her heavy energy needed a bit more coaxing than her other sisters to climb all the way up the golden spiral staircase to Iamone's moonlit space. Even though she was the most physically fit, Aneeda was content staying low on the ground level. She lived in a finite world of material things and thrived on her communal connections with everyone in Thisismeville. But sometimes that world could feel restrictive, and Aneeda would want to get a glimpse of what it might be like to feel light and free in the liberated space of Her Highness Sister Iamone's existence.

Every chakra sister did her part to help Aneeda begin the ascent. It took everyone focusing together to pull Aneeda's heaviness upward. Besides Ahafta's determination, there were only a few people in the family who could help lift the ground floor sister all the way up to Iamone's heights. Beloved Aunt Ida and Uncle Pingala could be counted on to help with this task. Whenever they came to visit the crystal castle, the chakra sisters knew that their cousin Oimalive would come along too. Oimalive could shake up the entire castle, always starting with Aneeda on the first floor.

Aunt Ida and Uncle Pingala had great knowledge and a special interest in the two golden spiral staircases that crisscrossed the center column of shimmering white light in the castle. Polishing the curving banisters and each golden plank in the staircases, Aunt Ida, Uncle Pingala, and Oimalive Fundalini made sure that the pathways up and down were unobstructed for the chakra sisters. They paved the way for the sisters to ascend quickly each day, connecting Aneeda all the way up to Iamone's floor, and back down again.

Oimalive and her parents had a mysterious background and an ancient, infamous family name–Fundalini. Rumor had it they descended from remote Himalayan relatives who were well versed in the trapeze arts. Others said they came from the womb of an earth goddess in a far-off corner of a lost continent called Shaktishivaland. Sometimes Aunt Ida and Uncle Pingala spoke of an ancient yogic practice that taught Oimalive how to initiate an intense internal dancing rite of passage, which is what all of the sisters needed to raise their vibrations, especially Aneeda.

Oimalive Fundalini had a slow, pleasant, serpentine type of energy. No one was ever sure when their unsuspecting, slinky cousin of Fundalini fame might show up. The seven sisters called this elusive cousin a divine goddess with magical life-giving powers. Aneeda just knew that whenever Oimalive came around and started to unwrap herself, sparks would fly and things would start to rumble in the castle.

A romantic legend told of young Oimalive's endless search for her beloved soul mate who lived in the stars.

The sisters loved embellishing her story.

"Oimalive's only desire is to reach Iamone's top floor of the castle."

"So she can fly out the uppermost windows . . ."

"And find her long-lost lover in the distant galaxies. Oh, I love that part," said Ahluvya.

"Where they will commingle forever in a union of enlightened bliss!" said Singya, her voice reaching a crescendo.

"I love that part about the commingling!" screamed Ivanna, leading her sisters into doubled-over laughter.

No matter how sacred an experience could be on Mt. Iknowmenow, the seven chakra sisters found a way to be a little irreverent in their spontaneous joy.

Oimalive Fundalini was a master flamethrower known for being able to control her breathing patterns, creating an energetic form of fire whose heat could rise to great heights, sometimes bursting through the ceiling. The chain of events ignited by Oimalive's first spark of life caused Aneeda to experience the transformative heat first. The force from this unique heat expanded upward, boiling Ivanna's water on the second floor. When the Fundalini fire hit Ahafta's solar panels on the third floor, the energy turned to steam.

As the steam moved up the castle floors, Ahluvya increased and stretched her breath, which turned the hot breezes blowing through her heart to vapor, and it rose up higher still to Singya's narrow hall-ways on the fifth floor. The hot vapor caused Singya to scream out a five-alarm warning, converting the vapor into energy which soared up to Useeme, who saw it transforming into intense heat waves of light. Speeding upward, this light woke up the entire top floor of the castle.

All of the flames, heated water, steam, vapor, hot air, wake-up signals, and bright light caused Iamone's mind to expand, burst-ing open and through her ceiling to an exquisite explosion of fire-works outside. All seven chakra sisters felt a blissful bioelectrical spark of life when this happened. There was an immediate sense of connecting to the vast universe, awakening them even more to the enlightened understanding and exuberant experience of unity with everyone and everything.

It didn't take long for the fireworks to turn downward, mov-ing back through the dark sky and into the clouds again. This in turn caused the bright light to move back down through Iamone's room and into the castle as if a downpour of hot, nourishing rain was washing over each sister.

The light of oneness flooded each sister's space, and they squealed "energia!" with renewed vigor and vitality. Whenever their cousin Oimalive Fundalini worked her magical fire energy in the crystal castle, the seven chakra sisters were filled with the deepest sense of knowing who they were as sparks of one divine universal cosmic light.

After the Fundalinis' visit, which was usually during a holiday, celebration, or long periods of meditation, the castle would shim-mer with a powerful, pleasant energy that felt full of life. Over time, the seven chakra sisters welcomed the Fundalini family into their home with open arms, knowing how wonderfully alive they would feel after their high frequency energetic explosions on pathways up and down the golden spiral staircases.

13
Meanwhile, Back on the Top Floor— The Manifesting Journey Begins

Iamone would have been happy to stay in her crowning position with the highest vantage point on Mt. Iknowmenow, deep in meditation and contemplation of her loving union with all of existence. But if she did, her batteries would run low without the energy of the Fundalinis and all her sisters below her.

In the beginning, the castle's energizing process was a two-way dance up and down the spiral staircase. All of the sisters needed to learn the steps in the proper order. Iamone's purpose was to receive the Queenking's spiritual messages for Mother Earth's people. But before any enlightened energy could be sent way down to the first floor, the other six chakra sisters first had to learn how to move their consciousness upward toward the freedom that awaited them in Iamone's room.

Like a spiritual cheerleader energized by cousin Oimalive, Iamone would allure her younger sisters up with her request:

> *Iamone is my name.*
>
> *Integration is my game.*

Come on up, we'll have some fun.

Feel the bliss, 'cause I-am-one!

But it wasn't that easy to get all the sisters to move upstairs at the same speed. Enlightenment sometimes felt like a chore that Iamone's little sisters resisted, and without Oimalive Fundalini's initial boost of energy it felt like the impossible waiting for a pot of water to boil. But indeed, they needed to learn the important up and down pathway for their individual energies to serve the whole castle.

Iamone's first preference was to invite her closest sister, Useeme, up to her heights so they could float together, poised and ready to drift off into flights toward new worlds of possibilities. When Iamone had an inspiring thought from the higher dimensions of the Queenking, she knew that Useeme would be able to envision it and see it clearly, to bring it into a picture that their sisters on the floors below could see and comprehend.

Once Useeme understood and drew the vision of Iamone's purposeful thought, she would call a council meeting in her command and control center of the castle. Inviting everyone up to sit in a circle under the Flower of Insight was a pleasure for Useeme, but it was sometimes a daunting task for the young ones below.

When they were younger, before they were coordinated but finally managed to gather together on the sixth floor, the sisters behaved like tiny birdlings, sticking out their tongues to drink the special liquid of enlightenment. They didn't know that the neck of the vase was positioned so it would drop directly onto the center of one forehead at a time, like it did with Useeme, not into their little eager mouths.

"One drop at a time girls, for one thought at a time. That's the only way the mind of our castle can function in perfection," reminded Useeme.

Useeme was patient and loving as she understood each of her sisters' efforts to maneuver her energy further up on the spiral staircase. She saw and appreciated that each sister had her own job to do in her own way, which was what made the entire castle run smoothly. After all, they were just beginning to learn the process of manifesting the castle's vitality, and it was up to Useeme to make it orderly.

After dismissing the sisters back to their own floors, Useeme let the elixir of insight soak deeply into her third eye and meditated herself into theta consciousness, where her subconscious mind could envision the whole plan for any given day. It didn't take long for the calming elixir to slow down her brain waves, first from her normally active beta brain waves to the slower and gentler alpha brain state where her awareness was alert but she was very relaxed. Here, Useeme would sink into the feeling she had when gazing at flickering candlelight. From this peaceful, meditative state Useeme drifted close to sleep but was still awake, enjoying the dreamy quality of even slower theta brain waves in her focused, receptive mind. This was her most creative state of being. In this state of theta consciousness, Useeme had mystical and psychic experiences where she held her unique perspective of Iamone's spiritual messages.

Next, the energy of the message would go down to the fifth floor for Singya to continue the process, expressing the idea into the entire castle. As Singya described Iamone's thought with her perfect words, the sisters below could hear it clearly, and it began to take on more meaning to everyone in the castle.

"OK sisters, listen up! You've gotta hear this. Iamone's been getting signals from the upper realms and she has another inspiring idea for the world's transformation."

From Singya's beautiful song, with just the right words and interpretations, Ahluvya felt the love from the heart of Iamone's original inspiration and breathing deeply, spread the hopeful energy down to Ahafta on the sunshine floor below.

On the breath of fresh air from the fourth floor, Ahafta would then infuse the idea with her specialized seasonings of sunshine valor, fiery courage, and hot fearlessness on the third floor.

Mixing Iamone's inspirations with Useeme's visions, Singya's explanations, and Ahluvya's exhalations, Ahafta's information began assimilating and digesting, and she passed it down one more floor. "I *have* to help all of us work this through to completion," said Ahafta. "There is nothing we cannot accomplish when we are in sync!"

With surety in her steps, Ahafta would run down the spiral staircase to the second floor where Ivanna received the transmissions next.

Ivanna had the skills to stir passions in the castle.

"Yes! I can *feel* it! I can practically taste it! Iamone, what a fabulous idea. I am filled with excitement and joy about our peaceful possibility manifesting in Thisismeville—and beyond! Let's have a party! I'm up for celebrating right now!"

"Hold on, little enthusiastic one. We have to include Aneeda or nothing can be accomplished."

Minding her own business being solid on the ground floor, Aneeda was happy looking through family photo albums, tending to her gardens, and pruning the trees. All of her needs were met and she was fulfilled and content. Satisfied with her lot in life, Aneeda laid down on the large red boulders in her living room to quietly rest. When she least expected it, an avalanche of energy from above unleashed and cascaded down into Aneeda's space. Being so energetically in touch with all her chakra sisters, this made her bolt upright with an overwhelming need to go outside and plant some seeds.

"OK, OK! I've got it! I need to grow Iamone's thought!" shouted Aneeda.

The sisters cheered as the reality hit that each had played her own particular part in the successful journey of an idea from Iamone to Aneeda's floor. As if she was being crushed with energy, Aneeda had no choice but to land feet first firmly on the ground.

The process of manifesting Iamone's inspiration translated as one magnificent flowing movement of energy through the castle. But Useeme knew that the sisters needed to practice daily to perfect the up-and-down dance into maturity.

14
The Journey Back Up the Castle Again— The Sisters Are Getting the Hang of It

Each chakra sibling had her own personality, likes and dislikes, talents and gifts, but eventually when they learned how to merge their energies together it created a vibrant life force that fused reality with fantasy. The seven sisters made sure that castle life on Mt. Iknowmenow was always an adventure for the inhabitants of Thisismeville, stretching everyone's imagination of what they thought was possible.

It took quite a bit of practice, but finally it became routine for Aneeda to start the daily process of connecting the sisters' bioenergetic spark plugs. The sisters learned from cousin Oimalive Fundalini that there had to be an equal amount of energy for the communication to travel from the ground floor up to the top and back down again. They understood the value of Useeme's orderly plan.

Every morning, as soon as the first redbirds began to sing outside Aneeda's window, she would awaken with clear eyes and eager anticipation of what another new day might bring. After a brisk walk in her gardens and a nourishing breakfast of roots and fruits,

Aneeda ran to the spiral staircase, remembering to activate her controlled Fundalini breathing.

To lighten up her heavy world of gravity and start her ascent to freedom, she headed up to Ivanna's floor with strong legs, a flexible back, and sturdy knees. She needed to ignite the six other engines that would run the castle each day. That's why she kept herself in excellent physical condition, making sure her joints were well lubricated and not stiff.

Reaching the second floor, Aneeda dipped her hand into the bowl of pumpkin seeds resting by Ivanna's front door. "Come on, Ivanna, stop primping! We need to connect with all of our sisters before we can start our day."

"I'm ready, Aneeda," said Ivanna, wiping fresh-squeezed orange juice off her lips and taking one more look at herself in the mirror. Adjusting her bustline and admiring her profile, she smoothed her copper-colored shirt down over her shapely hips and turned toward Aneeda. "How do I look?"

"Ivanna! It's morning meditation time. Who cares how you look?" Aneeda shook her head in dismay at how powerful the lure of the ego's vanity could be with her second floor sister.

Taking each other's hands, the earth and water sisters continued up the spiral staircase until they reached the beam of sunshine streaming into Ahafta's third floor foyer.

"It's always so hot in here, Ahafta!"

"Of course it is. I have to keep things cooking here in the castle!"

"And it's so bright on your sunny yellow floor," added Ivanna, admiring Ahafta's confident sense of her own personal power.

"Great! I love my brightness, so put on your sunglasses and look alert! We still have to climb some more," said Ahafta as she snuffed out the flame of her lemon-scented candle and pulled her sisters out the door of the third floor.

No matter how good their physical conditioning was, the morning trek to Ahluvya's open space on the fourth floor each day always made their breath quicken and their hearts race.

"Ahluvya, I *love* how it feels on your floor," said Aneeda.

"Like I can almost fly . . ." continued Ivanna.

"And soar like an eagle . . ." exclaimed Ahafta.

"Up into the sky!" laughed Ahluvya, finishing their spontaneous poetry.

Ahluvya plucked out six pink roses from her vase to share with her sisters and grabbed her green chiffon prayer shawl, tossing it around her neck as the four of them bounced their way up to the fifth floor.

The closer they got to Singya's cozy little quarters, the louder the sounds echoed inside the castle.

"Good morning, my little flying eagle sisters!" Singya called out. After greeting her sisters, Singya instinctively broke out in a song and encouraged the others to join in, to sing, chant, or simply say anything that would raise the vibrations and increase the energy at this height.

Getting slightly breathless while toning a string of *la-la-la-las, ma-mas,* and *ha-ha-ha-has,* they followed Singya's lead and kept going higher. Winding up and around the staircase, they could feel Useeme's space buzzing, which made their ears ring. Quieting their voices, they slowed their pace.

Useeme stood on her balcony and watched with keen eyes as her five little sisters approached. "I can see every move you make, sisters, so step lightly and stay in line!"

"OK, Eye Spy. We know, we know!"

The kaleidoscopic entry hall was always in process of changing colors and patterns. This was what the chakra princesses loved the most about reaching Useeme's floor. They stood in the middle of the two wings and saw a multitude of symbols, signs, shapes, and geometric designs in neon colors floating in front of their eyes. Sometimes, scenes of world situations or individuals with worn-out faces would go by, causing the sisters to consider the bigger picture of life. The visions on Useeme's floor always made them stop in fascination.

"Let's go," instructed Useeme. "Meditation practice starts now, girls. Be mindful as you take your sitting pillows into the Insight Chamber."

Useeme had learned quickly after those early experiments that it was much more efficient if she was the only one to receive the nectar from the Flower of Insight. Always eager to share her insights with her sisters, she guided them in every vision she received.

Quietly, Useeme coaxed each chakra sister to vividly imagine this day unfolding with each of her unique gifts adding to the whole.

A collective sigh followed after a long pause of silent gratitude, and the six chakra sisters stood up to continue their morning ritual upward to the seventh floor.

"Iamone knows she is connected to the divine all the time so meditation and prayer is not something she *does,* it's something she *is!*"

"Yes, and that is why and how we know who we are! Let's hear it for Iamone's wisdom. She keeps us in the light so our minds can stay connected to the higher mind of the universe."

"Really?" grinned Iamone as the others were just reaching the top of the stairs. "What you say makes me sound so . . . intense!" She calmly sat in the center of her giant lavender lotus blossom while all of her adoring sisters entered the room. Connecting with them gave Iamone her greatest sense of purpose and fulfillment.

"Are you ready to take your ego purifying bath now? It's been a long climb up here to the spiritual top. Remember little ones," continued the seventh sister with the sparkling amethyst and diamond crown, "there is an ego energy in our midst that is mischievous. It will always try to be the boss, telling you to stay away from me and the source of our energy. But you are the master, not the ego. Stay on track. You can never be separated from me! Remember that. Keep your focus on living a spiritual life by being kind to yourself and in loving service to all. Only then can abundant goodness be ours to enjoy every day." It was a message that Iamone told the sisters each morning. They never got tired of hearing this from their enlightened sister on the top floor.

"We're ready!"

Eagerly, the seven chakra princess sisters climbed way up on top of Iamone's huge lotus covered bedspread and got in line. Iamone opened the skylights overhead even wider to accommodate a blast of cosmic white light that poured over them. They anticipated this ceremony from their angelic sister every morning, but the light still seemed blinding at certain moments.

After a long while of silently receiving the nourishing divine light, they were filled with the Big Love, as if they were being renewed by the entire universe. This act of receiving gave them a new way of perceiving that always opened the gates for unexpected miracles to happen.

"Cleansed!" declared Aneeda.

"Grateful!" affirmed Ivanna, Ahafta, and Ahluvya.

"Purified!" sang Singya.

"Blessed," sighed Useeme and Iamone.

Their checklist was complete. They were free! With the understanding that they needed to pay attention to the ego's incessant distractions by meditating this way, they felt refreshed, comfortable, and ready to start another new day.

"Thanks, Iamone! You're the best big sister in the entire cosmos!"

Joy was the dominant vibration on the top floor of the castle, and Iamone's pure happiness made the whole castle smile. "Sisters, our job today is to fully share the light that just fed us so well. We must let it spill over to others. And with love, just witness what they choose to do with it, like the Queenking does with us." Iamone's advice flowed outward with ease and beauty. She was like a divine mother, loving her sisters as she would precious children.

As if they had just digested a royal breakfast of spiritual energy and awareness, the seven chakra sisters were now wide awake and more alert than ever. Now, without having to go through all the steps of bringing the vibrations down to each floor one at a time, they knew their mission. Running to the slick and sparkling banisters of the golden spiral staircases, they took turns jumping on and sliding down, swirling with grace and speed all the way to the bottom floor.

"Watch me! Look out, here I come!"

"*Whiiizzzzzz...*"

"Look at the red trail Aneeda made down the stairs. She's moving so fast!"

Exhilarated screams of giddiness erupted from seven rainbow streaks of light.

"Don't make me laugh or I'm gonna pee."

"Whoa—the castle is blurring past me!"

"Ha! I love this! It feels like I'm snowboarding!" shouted Ahafta, her blonde mane flying straight out behind her.

Every day was a new opportunity for the seven chakra sisters to make sure the castle was running smoothly. Eventually they learned how to move together as one reliable unit when it came to serving others as well, whether it was hosting a gala for the entire population of Thisismeville or organizing an international conference on feeding the hungry. The chakra sisters were passionate and had a deep desire to help those in need. After their morning visits with Iamone, they were spiritually primed and prepared to face the challenges of the earthly world of humanity. They were ready to transform their awareness into productive action!

Running out the front door of the castle, the seven chakra sisters carried the energy of the universe's ultimate messages out into the big world.

Today, there was a consensus. Looking at each other with eager anticipation, they all agreed. "Yep, it's time to throw the biggest party Thisismeville has ever seen!"

15
A Grand Festival—
The 7 Chakra Sisters
Work as a Team

The chakra sisters existed in a mystical metaphysical realm, beyond the physical world. They drifted through experiences of timelessness while still maneuvering gravity on earth, sensing their energy warping past linear time. After a few more phenomenal visits from their cousin Oimalive Fundalini, they were feeling more mature with each boost of her energy, and they shifted into ageless wonders. The sisters knew who they were as eternal energetic beings, timeless and formless, so they had fun testing their abilities to converge the worlds of dense humanity, time, space, and boundaries with the freedom, lightness, and limitlessness of soul. A grand festival was the perfect opportunity.

The excitement and bustle of planning a party for their friends in Thisismeville thrilled the seven chakra sisters, and each did her part, following her own unique qualities for collectively manifesting their first grand festival in the town. Iamone was already blessing the idea of an all-inclusive town gathering where everyone would feel the joy of collaborating for the purpose of celebrating life.

Useeme could envision the party in its entirety, making sure that the details and plans of every component were drawn out for the team to implement without a hitch. Like a master architect, she shared her visions with the sisters underneath her, knowing they would carry them out to completion.

Since a festival like this had never been done before, Singya began spreading the word to all of her friends in Thisismeville and listened for their feedback. She prepared the grounds with her high vibrations by chanting for the angels-in-charge-of-wild-frolicking to watch over the area.

Singya communicated with the sound technicians and invited all the local bands to perform music of every culture. Five hundred drummers would play their intricately designed djembes and doumbeks underlain with Turkish brass and Egyptian mother-of-pearl. Singers, master chanters, rappers, jazz musicians, blues groups, and operatic singers would fill the airways around Mt. Iknowmenow. Speakers would deliver soliloquies, educators would give presentations, actors would recite poetry, and poets would recite monologues.

Ahluvya balanced her sisters' relationships, so the party planning would be easy. Her heart center's loving vibrations pulled the townspeople into the exciting energies that expanded around the castle during the preparations. She imported four hundred rose-winged parakeets and exactly four thousand emerald green hummingbirds to create a magnificent flutter effect over the party meant to fill the air with a Lightness of being and the soft flurry of a beating heart.

Ahafta's confidence gave all the sisters permission to dream big. She ordered three thousand monarch butterflies to grace the treetops, continuing the lighthearted energy that Ahluvya had planned, and manifested three thousand yellow canary-shaped candles to adorn the tables. She also arranged to have hot coals for the firewalkers and encircled the flamethrowers with three hundred medieval torchères to highlight their effectiveness. Ahafta started huge bonfires in each zone of activity so the guests could have light and warmth after the sun set.

Ivanna's party-planning enthusiasm was contagious, and she set the mood for the festivities. If Ivanna was happy, everyone was happy. The second floor chakra sister adored playing with the color schemes and textures that would bring creativity and life to the party. Fountains of fresh-squeezed orange juice were placed between massive pillars of water that sprayed out like sparkling liquid fireworks. Ivanna after all, was the juiciest sister, and she carried an aura of sweetness into all of her activities.

Being the lover of liquids, Ivanna was also responsible for setting up the water sports section of the festival. Dolphins from the local seaside were imported to the massive pools in the castle's courtyard. She made sure that waterways, like curving roads, flowed through every festive area and provided bright copper gondolas to transport guests wherever they wanted to go.

Next in line, Aneeda focused on maintaining the grounds around Mt. Iknowmenow where the gathering would take place. She arranged for edible gardens to cover the fields on the east side of the mountain and soft, earthy red sand to be laid on all the walking paths to the west side, bordered by large, polished bloodstones.

Hosting an event like this was a perfect outlet for Aneeda's otherwise sedentary tendencies. She worked in tandem with all of her sisters, planning to set the buffet tables with hand-painted ruby clay plates from Red River rock down the road. The grounded sister made sure that the feast included red potatoes, red cabbage, red peppers, rhubarb, and everything with roots that could be eaten. She suggested that watermelons be served on red quartz platters, garnished with bright strawberries, raspberries, cherries, and crimson cranberries.

So extravagant would this festival be, that the princesses hired a full circus to be escorted by seventy lively white horses with shining black manes and then perform high over the banquet tables as their guests enjoyed their meal.

Because they were so at ease with themselves and their friends, the seven sisters decided in the future that they would have many lavish feasts and banquets to welcome and greet everyone in their radiant royal land. They lived in a consciousness of abundance. Their appreciation for the unlimited goodness of life spilled over to all who were in their presence, lifting everyone around them.

Not since the castle lights had turned on with the birth of the seven chakra princess sisters had the townspeople of Thisismeville felt so invigorated. This would be the grand gathering of all of their sublime energy.

16
A Secret Ceremony—
The Chakra Sisters
Have Sweet Memories

A week before the actual festival was to begin, the seven chakra sisters decided to participate in a special ceremony. They knew their intentions of hosting a gala with the highest vision and purpose of generously loving their friends in Thisismeville would be anchored by a ceremony, if for no reason other than celebrating the joy of being alive.

Taking a break from their party planning process, the sisters, shrouded in sacred secrecy, met at the bottom of the golden spiral staircase at midnight. Making sure they each had what they needed they headed out the huge rose quartz front doors of the castle with their flashlights and oil lanterns, deep into the moss-covered bog, damp and thick with the moisture of the night air. The sisters trekked with their old boots and torn jeans. Some had tattered gloves, while others donned shredded wool shawls or tight-knit hats pulled down to their eyebrows. These were their favorite to clothes to wear in the disguise of night when their princess personas could be left behind for the adventure ahead.

They could see their breath in the chilly night air. The sky was lit by a full Mother Moon, which cast a pearlescent blue light on the old trees and caused a shadow in the background of the forest floor. Soft brown pine needles crunched lightly beneath their boots.

They could see the dried sap glistening from the bark of the ancient trees in the silver moonlight. Together, they asked for permission and said a prayer before delicately scraping off the sticky substance that would be used later for the sacred fire.

The dense forests that surrounded Mt. Iknowmenow were a second home to the seven sisters. It was here that they learned the healing ways of the elementals of earth, water, fire, and air. The magical woods also introduced them to the mystical realm of benevolent faeries, wood nymphs, and other supernatural beings.

Useeme and Iamone preferred the less dense world of light and thought but appreciated their other sisters' needs to connect with physical matter. All of the sisters felt safe to explore the world in these woods. Usually they traveled together on all of their adventures, but sometimes there was a rare exception.

"I swear I floated at least six inches off the ground that day." Aneeda told her favorite story every time they reached this point in the forest, but her sisters always humored her.

"This path was soft under my bare feet, even though you can see it's made of small, rough pebbles," she recalled. "I have never run so fast in my life! It felt fantastic! I was flying. . . . I was free!"

Although Aneeda was intent on staying physically fit and healthy in every way, she was the slowest moving and heaviest of all her sisters. She shivered as she recounted the day of her unexpected adventure in the woods, when she was wild with courage and practically elevated while on her run down the path.

"After I crossed the little wooden bridge at the crook of the creek, right over there, I sat down between the twin pines and waited for one of my earth elemental friends to show up. I was watching the sunlight dance on the water when suddenly the tiny King Faerie formed before my eyes, rising right out of the stream!"

"Do you think we might see him tonight?" asked her sisters, knowing full well that Aneeda just wanted to tell her story and not discuss the King Faerie's possible appearance on this particular evening.

She continued, "There he was, as clear as I'm seeing you now. He raised his little arm up above his tiny royal head and kept pointing to the west, somewhere just over my left shoulder. He was shaking and pointing frantically. He wanted me to look at something!

"I was crouched on the ground by then, mesmerized by the King Faerie. I wasn't really paying attention to what he wanted me to see; I was just staring at him gesturing wildly."

"Aneeda, do you think he was just waving to say hello to you?" asked Ivanna, even though she had already heard how this story ended many times.

"No! He had an important message for me!"

Patiently, Aneeda's sisters waited for her to continue.

"Finally, I realized that I should look in the direction he wanted me to."

"You mean you didn't feel like going into fight or flight or freeze mode?" asked Ahafta, feigning astonishment. Aneeda was the sister who had the strongest primordial tendencies to stay in survival mode, no matter how she did it.

"No! I was brave and anchored my energy down my legs and into my feet."

"What happened next, Aneeda?"

"The King Faerie was shaking by now, urgently wanting me to look at something. It had to be behind me. So, slowly I turned around . . ." The rooted chakra sister was relishing the attention she was getting. She learned well from Singya's little games how to keep everyone in suspense, although she was not nearly as dramatic as Ivanna would have been.

"Aneeda," encouraged Ahafta, "we must be at the campfire before the sun rises. Please tell us the end of the story!"

"Oh, yes. Well, as I sloooowly turned to look over my left shoulder, I could only see the endless rows of pine trees behind me. I looked back to the King Faerie and now his small ten-inch body was hovering over the stream, his angst increasing in intensity. My heart was pounding!"

"A ten-inch faerie? You've got to be kidding."

"What?! What did he want you to see, Aneeda!?" demanded Singya.

When Singya spoke out loud, it caused all the night critters of the forest to begin their chorus of chirps, clicks, and squeaks. Frogs croaked. Crickets buzzed. Hoot owls twirbled. Everyone in the forest was now wide awake and paying close attention to Aneeda's story.

"Well, I began to look around and at first I didn't see anything unusual. But then I looked up. And right over my face, as close as the hat on my head, was a giant web and a massive—no, a *goliath*—hairy black spider!"

Her sisters spontaneously gasped, audibly enough to encourage Aneeda's enthusiastic storytelling.

"But, Aneeda, you love all of nature's creatures, right?"

"Yes, I do, but not if they are going to kill me!" Aneeda's greatest need of all, more than any of her other sisters, was to stay alive!

"Sweet Aneeda," said Iamone in her usual calm and wise manner, "there is no such thing as death, only transformation from one form into another."

The rest of the siblings had heard Iamone's counsel so many times they blatantly ignored her spiritual admonishments this time.

"So what happened next, Aneeda? Did the big, black, spooky spider jump on your head? And creeeep down your neck?" With that, the sisters became very animated and started dancing around Aneeda, touching her hair with their pointed fingers, mimicking the King Faerie.

Aneeda was used to this playful exchange but pushed her sisters away in a show of strength. "No, it never had a chance. I was too swift and took off like a racehorse out of the gate. That's when I knew I could run so fast I could lift off, like a peregrine falcon or a jumbo jet!"

With that, Aneeda tore off down the path ahead of her sisters. Laughter filled the forest until it awakened the ground beneath their feet. Mother Earth was rumbling and the night animals were grumbling. The sisters knew they had better move on quickly. Now, all seven of them were racing away from the little bridge, grinding the tiny pebbles into the soles of their boots with every pounding step. Their lanterns were swinging in every direction, causing a gross distortion of the trees surrounding them. Shrieking with joy, they ran breathlessly into the clearing where the ceremony would take place before sunrise.

They had been at this particular place only once before, on their fifth birthday. It was to be the year before their little subconscious minds were conditioned with the proper programming for life. The intention for that ceremony long ago was to seal the memory of their internal and eternal power into their consciousness.

Each sister stood at the edge of the clearing now, their breaths slowing down as they remembered that precious night when they turned five years old. Since there was no dimension of time in the enchanted lands around Mt. Iknowmenow, the sisters felt as though they had stepped right back into the living memory of that moment.

It was nighttime when they were taken to a sacred fire in this field, created by their adoring ancestors. Maidens and goddesses had simply appeared without any announcements or distinguishing actions. The handmaidens took precious care that evening as they dressed each princess sister. Silken, luminous fabrics were slowly and meticulously draped over their bodies in preparation for their initiations. They were being enveloped in both earthly and heavenly energy.

A large masculine figure wearing a headdress of exotic feathers slowly approached the young sisters. His eyes were the color of rich brown soil, and when he looked deeply into another's eyes he pierced anything which stood in the way of direct contact with their soul. The priest held a radiant crystal wand in his right hand which contained the records of the children's infinite lifetimes. In his left hand, he held a small leather pouch filled with a special resin that would be thrown upon the sacred fire at just the right moment. The high shaman priest called them the Beautiful Ones.

A wisdom keeper took the hands of each small child and led them to a massive stone altar in the center of the expansive field. One by one, they were hoisted high up onto the altar by strong guardians and were told to stand in a line, starting with Aneeda and ending with Iamone. The girls were curious but unafraid. Their trust in sacred ceremonies was well established in their young hearts.

Rattles, bells, and gentle drumming in the background enhanced the atmosphere of this indigenous setting. The sisters felt they were communicating telepathically with nature and all the wildlife around them.

They listened as the shaman spoke an unspoken language, praying over a small clay bowl. He placed the crystal wand of lifetime memories tenderly on an amethyst stand and kept his hand over it for a brief moment, as if to place a protective energy into the wand for safekeeping.

The high priest then tossed the resin from his leather pouch into the flames of the sacred fire, causing a wide spray of opalescent lights to burst up into the night sky. It was a signal to their original starseed family that the ceremony had begun.

He held up seven large black feathers and dipped the tips into the clay container that held his silent prayers. Firelight blazed into the sisters' eyes as they watched the tall silhouette begin to dance across the stone floor. He began slowly, taking deliberate steps in a circle around each sister. The drumming was more deliberate now and his feet matched the steady rhythm.

The seven sisters looked at one another with wide eyes, remembering to show respect for this particular elder. They stood very still as the shaman dancer began to twirl faster and faster around them. The feathers became extensions of his hands, and it appeared as if he might take flight any moment. He turned into a soaring hawk and spread his long arm-wings over the heads of the little girls.

They didn't need to understand what the actions meant; they just received the blessings with gratitude. They were already familiar with what they could see beyond their physical eyes, and shapeshifting seemed normal in the lands of Mt. Iknowmenow.

The priest slowed his dance and transformed back into his human figure. He once again dipped the feathers into an old earthen vessel which held a shiny gold pigment. With the ceremonial feathers, he began to paint each tiny face. First their cheeks, then across their forehead, down their nose, and completely covering their ears. The wet tips of the feathers tickled the girls, but they held back from giggling. In that moment, the seven chakra sisters remembered their soul contracts with the ancient wisdom keepers.

Voices filled the night sky around the circle. The light of the fire cast shadows behind all the people, and in unison they whispered in soft song-chant tones, "Welcome home. Welcome home. You are one of us now." The chakra princesses were filled with excitement because they knew they were one with this loving community, the Tribe of All-Knowing, which held the quintessential energy of every particle and wave that ever existed throughout the universes. When the ceremony was completed the seven sisters realized that they would always remember their natural state of being. They embraced the transcendental bliss of their unity with the consciousness of all things.

Reminiscing over the time when they were so young, they felt humbled for the love that was poured on them when they were first initiated into their cosmic tribe. Now, at the edge of the clearing, Aneeda could still feel her bare feet standing on the coolness of the smooth stone alter from that night long ago. Ivanna remembered the pungent scents of the fire, burning with white sage and copal. Ahafta remembered the strong sense of personal power in the center of her body as the shaman priest initiated her with the gold-tipped feathers. Ahluvya's heart opened wide and she took a deep breath of gratitude as she reminisced about their sacred ceremony and loved how connected she felt to everyone in their Tribe of All-Knowing. Singya recalled all the sounds of the night's event . . . the crackling of the fire, the humming of the trees swaying around them, how angelic and deep the tribes people's voices sounded as they chanted their welcoming songs. Useeme saw clearly in her mind the vivid colors of the night shapes and how the smoke swirled the prayers upward in curling ribbons that rose out of the yellow-white fire. And Iamone remembered who she was on that night and on this night, as she and her sisters entered another realm of spiritual ritual once again.

"I love this magical place," sighed Ahluvya.

"Come on, sisters, let's go. We have to get ready. These memories are great, but we have another ceremony waiting for us now." Ahafta's fiery nudge reminded everyone to get moving.

Tonight, the seven chakra sisters would be initiated into the next level of purification. Their consciousness was evolving as they matured, and they looked forward to another boost in the energy they carried within them. This time, the sisters had the intention to prepare themselves with the right attitude for the grand festival ahead.

They placed their lanterns on the damp grass and began to take off their boots, holey caps, and frayed gloves.

"We'll need to bathe in the cleansing pools tonight, so fire up the heat in your gut, girls!" Ahafta always seemed to have the energy needed to stoke the flames that burned within them. She made sure that she kept the motivation high whenever they were on a specific assignment.

"But I'm hungry!" moaned Aneeda.

"And I'm feeling a little aroused," laughed Ivanna.

"Restrain yourself, Ivanna. We love your spontaneous wildness, but you will have to stifle your emotional urges for now. We have a job to do, so let's not get distracted," said Ahafta, always maintaining her presence with integrity.

Ahluvya was sighing aloud now, feeling her heart swell with love for her sisters. She accepted them just the way they were—hungry, horny, and humble.

"I feel a celebratory song coming on!"

"Shhh, Singya," chided her sisters. "Every time you sing, you know what happens. You shake up the surroundings and change the vibrations of everything around us."

"That's the plan though, right Useeme?" Singya was always looking to her "older" sister for the sign that her singing was appropriate in certain situations.

"Sing to your heart's content, Singya, but let's respect Ahafta's reminders to stay on track."

⁓

Tonight would be a simple celebration ceremony to energize the sisters as the festival approached. Their extended Tribal family of All-Knowings encircled them once again, dancing and drumming to the heartbeat of life, causing the sacred fire to leap in wild bursts of incandescence.

The Beautiful Ones laughed within an aura of enchantment when a familiar figure came flying down, surprising them from the high canopy of trees in this ancient land. It swooped up the seven sisters and headed toward the stars. Their ceremonial silk gowns flowed and flapped right along with the powerful feathered wings of their dearest guardian friend and teacher, Owl Woman. They rode into the moon shadows and back again, feeling energized and enlivened. As the winds blew into their memories, they inhaled stardust and abundant joy. The seven chakra sisters were in synchronistic harmony with everything around them.

When they finally landed back at the sacred fire, the sisters were given strings of tiny bells which they tied around their ankles. The soft bells jingled as they danced, matching the distant calls of the crickets in the dark surrounding fields, and they celebrated into the night while the drummers from their Tribe of All-Knowing kept a steady rhythm.

The seven chakra sisters learned well from their wise teachers about the intrinsic value of these sacred, magical, and meaningful ceremonies. Tonight, they had fully anchored their purpose of sharing peaceful oneness with the world. It would all start in Thisismeville.

17

The Festival Flows as It Comes and Goes—All Is Well in Thisismeville

On the day of the festival, their favorite cousin Oimalive Fundalini unexpectedly showed up in the castle as the sisters were getting dressed. Just being in her powerful presence caused the seven chakra sisters to completely surrender their open hearts to the sweetest love of all. They were spinning in ecstasy and filled with excitement. Grace filled their space.

The gala didn't have a specific starting time. It just gradually came about, like the changing colors of an awakening dawn sky. All of the families from neighboring villages came to enjoy the brilliant rainbow-colored lights that were radiating from all seven floors of the crystal castle. There was a feeling of simplicity and tranquility in the atmosphere around Mt. Iknowmenow.

Without any special proclamation, the seven chakra princess sisters slipped out the front door of their home and quietly melted into the crowds. They felt a deep union with everyone and shared a natural appreciation for the miracle of life and humanity in Thisismeville.

The varied paths of sand, moss, canals, and candlelight were laid around the grounds, and the guests leisurely walked, rode, or glided to each area of earth, water, or fire. A perfect cool breeze balanced the warm air and carried the party music throughout the festival. The essence of pure ease and friendship followed the people in every direction. At every turn the mood shifted with the unique smells, sounds, and sights of the celebration.

The seven chakra sisters had created a magnificent merging of royalty with reality. They were ebullient on the outside while remaining calm and still inside. Each sister knew she had done her specific task with diligent excellence and it felt effortless.

The festival never actually had an ending time either. The townspeople drifted in and out of the castle grounds, enjoying the festive feelings for what felt like endless days. The good mood and the extraordinary flow of abundance just kept moving onward into cycles of timelessness, which was natural for the chakra sisters' metaphysical existence. There was plenty of food, entertainment, creativity, and camaraderie. People fell in love. Babies were born. Children advanced in all skills. People became generous and cooperative with each other. New life-enhancing innovations were launched. Everyone shared in the sustainable caring of the land, and nutritional community gardens were planted. New galaxies were discovered. Science and magic merged. World peace ensued.

By the end of the seventh day, the angels-of-having-a-blast-forever whispered to the chakra sisters that even Creation needed to rest. It was time to end the party and take the dolphins back to their natural habitat. Captivity was never on the agenda for their friends of the sea. A multitude of horses and butterflies were also set free from the castle grounds. It was understood that respect for all living things was paramount.

There were other festival activities that began to wind down as well. The acrobats began to dismantle their high-wire beams and trapeze nets, and the bonfires were reduced to embers. Candles burned out, napkins were folded, and the fountains of orange juice slowed to a trickle.

The townspeople felt their hearts open when the song birds were allowed to find their own place again in the wild. In a magnificent whoosh of wings, their chorus echoed farther and farther away into the skies over Thisismeville, signaling to all that the grand festival was finally coming to a gentle close.

18
Sweet Dreams
for the Sisters—
Or the Beginning
of a Nightmare?

The sisters reveled in their accomplishment and happily went to their rooms for a much-needed rest after the week-long party. But first, they gathered in Iamone's room where a prayer of gratitude was said for all the good fortune that seemed to continually bless the crystal castle in every moment. Then, one by one, the sisters went down to their floors and found their favorite spot to settle down for the night.

On the seventh floor, Iamone lifted herself onto her lavender lotus blossom bed and felt herself float up and out of her skylights, directly into the stars above her and then into the vastness of space beyond. She felt the oneness shared by all who had experienced the festival and knew that all was well in the castle on Mt. Iknowmenow.

On the sixth floor, Useeme sat on her oversized meditation pillow and placed a soft indigo mask over her eyes. Soon she could see vivid geometric patterns of purple and red checkerboard squares which grew large enough in her mind to engulf her completely in brilliant white light. In an instant, right before her brain moved into the delta frequencies of sleep, Useeme knew this would be a perfect canvas for creating imaginative dream images.

On the fifth floor, Singya laid down to feel the vibrations on her circular turquoise blue sound bed and chanted along with the vibrations of deep sleep mantras.

On the fourth floor, Ahluvya opened her windows to see the last of the hot air balloons descending over the distant mountains. Then she tumbled into her green air bed. Her heart was wide open and she filled herself with an exquisite vibration of love for everyone she knew and didn't know.

On the third floor, Ahafta got comfortable on her golden-yellow bed of fire and felt the warm glow of confidence move through her midsection. She was empowered with the thought of how well she could manifest anything and was proud of herself for achieving her goals.

On the second floor, Ivanna took a long, luxurious bubble bath, put on her orange laced nightgown, and bobbed on her warm water bed. Satisfied feelings washed over her as she drifted off to dreamland, filled with gladness that she had so many friends in her life.

Self-sufficient Aneeda laid on her solid red rock boulder, which was the most comfortable bed in her first floor room. Grounded with a sense of abundance and prosperity, and feeling safe and secure, Aneeda provided the foundation for all her sisters resting in their rightful places.

On their own floors of the castle, the seven chakra sisters were breathing in synchronistic rhythm. Satisfied with the harmony that everyone was experiencing, the sisters gently closed their energy down for the night. They fell asleep to dream in pleasant peacefulness, completely unaware that there was a dark force lurking in their land.

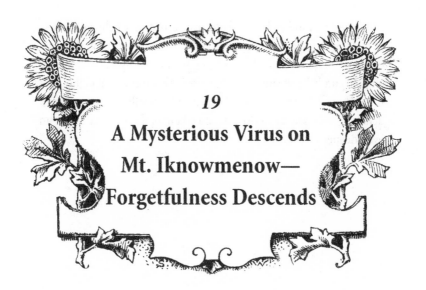

19

A Mysterious Virus on
Mt. Iknowmenow—
Forgetfulness Descends

After the grand festival, the obligatory ominous cloud of uh-oh-here-comes-trouble slowly began to drift toward the peaks of Mt. Iknowmenow.

While the sisters were sleeping, a foreboding energy came seeping through the windowsills, depositing an invisible blast of fateful air under the doorways. This new creeping nemesis would change everything in the crystal castle and eventually Thisismeville.

It was not the norm for any of the sisters to leave the castle alone. They went everywhere together, only separating for brief moments if they wanted to take a private stroll in nature close to the immediate grounds of Mt. Iknowmenow. But they were always within close proximity to each other and mostly lived their lives happily together inside the castle.

This night, Aneeda had fallen into a lovely lucid dream. In her altered state, she was spending an unusually long time in the woods, taking turns chasing squirrels and then lying under the shade of the massive redwoods. While on her back feeling grounded and supported by Mother Earth, frogs leaped over her belly and grasshoppers jumped on her legs. Her friends, snake and slug, slithered over her hair, and Aneeda had thoughts of the organic red lettuce and burgundy beets she would harvest for her dinner salad that evening. She dug her fingers into the rich soil beneath her and breathed deeply. Inside this vivid dream, Aneeda happily drifted off into an even deeper level of sleep.

20
The Spell of Fear—
Aneeda Encounters
Fergetcha
Kundameanie

A needa's dream within a dream gave her a soft, pleasurable sense of peace, and her imagination flourished in her dream world on this innocent lazy afternoon when, without warning, something odd crept into the corner of her lucid awareness. A thick, shadowy shape was quickly approaching her. Aneeda's trust in the good nature of life usually supported her wherever she went, but this particular stranger startled her, which in itself startled her even more, since she was normally so solid and secure in her surroundings.

"Who are you? I don't remember ever seeing you in these woods."

"Well, little princess," a raspy voice replied, "I wouldn't expect that you would remember me. I am Fergetcha!"

Deeper into the dream she fell, until Aneeda couldn't tell if she was actually asleep or awake. Aneeda forced a small sound out of her mouth, "What? Who? . . . Ferwhatta?"

This caused Fergetcha to howl with laughter. "*Fergetcha!* Hear me loud and clear, miss princess Aneeda. I am the master of

Kundameanie energy . . . Fergetcha Kundameanie is my name. Pain and misery is my game. I am the powerful force that stops everything from growing. I am the worst part of the hidden darkness of your ego. Once you meet me, you will meet endless difficult challenges . . . and you will forget all you ever knew about your happy little life in your colorful castle!"

Fergetcha's diabolical laughter filled the woods, which caused all the animals, creepy crawlies, and winged ones to scatter.

Aneeda was in a state of shock. Was she dreaming? She couldn't move.

"You silly child. You think you've got it all together, don't you? You spoiled, privileged princess, you. You think you have everything you need, don't you?" Aneeda's heart started to pound as the barrage continued.

"You and your prissy organic gardens under your big solid feet. Talking so sweetly to the critters out here, learning about my stone's secret ways, hanging out in *my* forest."

Aneeda was shaking by now, never having heard such a grating vibrational tone in anyone's voice. Fergetcha's twisted face was now nose to nose with Aneeda's.

"This land was mine before you and your family brought all those bright shiny lights into my neighborhood. You've taken from me ever since you arrived here—my food, my water. My land has given you shelter and safety . . . but no more! You're taking up my space. You have no right to be here! I want you and your perfect little namby-pamby sisters gone! I am taking it back. This territory is *mine!*" Fergetcha lurched forward and grabbed Aneeda's shoulders.

Aneeda's body tightened as she fell even deeper into an unknown foggy world. Not knowing if this nightmare was real or not, she began to cry, descending into a despair that the rooted chakra sister had never felt before. Her surroundings began to change. Her special grandmother tree began shapeshifting into a hideous monster with glaring, bulging eyes; it was reprimanding her for something . . . but what? No one had ever spoken to her in this way.

"You can never be satisfied, Aneeda, can you? You need the perfect foods. You need your warm blankie. You need people around you so you can feel like you belong to a tribe, with all of their false new ways of being. Can't even stand on your own two feet, can you? Face it, you're just a weak little *needy* princess, Aneeda! You can't do anything on your own!"

Aneeda heard Fergetcha's wicked words, but she could only see the edges of a dark swirling shape around her. Aneeda shuddered as the menacing movements filled her with fear for the first time in her life.

"It was my ancestors who survived for eons out here in this cold, hard world. It was my tribe that wrestled with all the unknown, unpredictable dangers. It has always been a struggle for people like me! We were the ones who had to battle the pain of oppression or the fears of being trampled or eaten by wild, mad predators. The Kundameanie family has only known fear and suffering. It's the only way we know how to survive. And we won't change it now with you and your sisters' high-falutin' spiritual practices!"

Fergetcha's rampage caused Aneeda to recoil, but the old hag continued. "My Kundameanie clan has lived in victimhood forever, and we will not let you or your sisters take our pain away from us! I have always felt deprived, and now so shall you! There is not enough food for all of us. I know scarcity! That's the reality of things. There is never enough of anything. Not enough food, not enough money, never enough happiness. I have always had to fight for what's mine! You and your creepy little sisters are taking up my precious space and I am taking it back, now!"

Blasting her last warning, she screamed, "You are not safe here in this big, scary world, Aneeda! You will never be safe again, now that you know me. Be prepared to be severed from all that you know, miss earthy princess! No one wants you around, especially me." With a swoosh, Fergetcha was gone.

Aneeda was suddenly jerked awake from this unspeakable double nightmare and found herself alone in the woods. The chilled predawn air caused her teeth to chatter and a tremble shook deep from within her bones. Shaking and alone, the first chakra princess felt the pain of fear grip her body. Fergetcha Kundameanie's words lingered like rancid smoke in her head.

Adjusting her disbelieving eyes, she looked around, slowly taking in her surroundings. "How did I get here? What just happened!?" Aneeda only knew that she was no longer on her favorite red rock in the castle. Her feet seemed to be disconnected from her wobbly legs as she tried to stand. She felt unsure of herself and unstable in what used to be familiar territory. Even simple noises from the timid night animals sounded harsh and shrill. She felt alienated from everything and could not understand this feeling of being separated from her sisters and the castle. Her memory of them was fading quickly.

Fergetcha observed all this from behind some wild strawberry plants that once used to bring sweet red pleasures to Aneeda. Her condemning energy caused the plump fruits to immediately turn brown and droop their heads. She bared her crooked teeth with a cunning smile as she watched Aneeda grope her way through the thicket in the woods toward Mt. Iknowmenow. Uprooted and in a daze, Aneeda forgot where she was going or where she was supposed to be. She was forgetting all that she had known so far in her royal lifetime.

Fergetcha Kundameanie slowly voiced her vow: "I have lived here since this mountain started as a little bump hill. This is my stomping ground where my job is to cause pain and misery to all the townspeople and little critters on this land! I hate change! I like what is familiar and you sisters are strangers here. I can't stand to be around this new lovey-dovey energy from some big divine source. My aim is to keep what is mine and to destroy anything that threatens my world. I won't let you change my comfort zone or allow your sickening spiritual sweetness to take away my fun. I've come back to collapse your menacing castle, once and for all, one floor at a time, if that's what it takes to finally get things back to the way they used to be."

Aneeda stumbled, landing facedown over a rough tree root.

"When you and your chakra sisters forget who you are," gloated Fergetcha, "then I will rule this kingdom once again!"

In the distance, the morning sun reflected off the large windows on the front of the castle. The light nearly blinded Aneeda, but she was drawn to it. For a fleeting moment there was something that felt secure and comforting about seeing that bright light. However, the first floor of the castle seemed unusually darker than the others as she approached it on this particular day.

The crystal castle's drawbridge was up. No one in the castle knew that Aneeda had been gone for a whole night, and Aneeda had no idea how long she had been gone herself. This terrifying experience had robbed her of all sense of time and order to her life.

The base of Mt. Iknowmenow seemed outrageously huge and far away, but Aneeda managed to make her way back to the pink quartz doors and into the first floor of the castle. As she entered the foyer she had a vague recollection of seeing that red convertible sports coupe parked in her hall foyer before, but she had no idea why it was there.

"Wow, who decorated this place?" Aneeda thought to herself. "A little overdone with the red color, I'd say." Then she noticed her swollen feet. They ached, and it was hard for her to stand even for a few minutes.

"I don't feel very well . . . ouch!" Aneeda moaned to herself, rubbing a bump on her bruised shins. "What happened to my legs? They feel so tired and heavy. . . . And my knees . . . I can barely move them. What's happening to me?"

Aneeda had already completely forgotten about yesterday's festival and her unfortunate encounter with Fergetcha during the night. Never having had any experience with this kind of fear, Aneeda's body began to shake uncontrollably. She had no idea that an evil spell of forgetfulness had been cast upon her. She felt weak and unsure of taking one step farther, and this made her even more afraid. Panic shot through her body and she passed out, dropping like a dead red brick on the imported scarlet carpet.

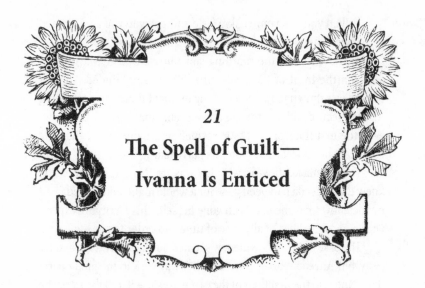

21

The Spell of Guilt—
Ivanna Is Enticed

As the sun rose higher, Fergetcha was reveling in the success of capturing Aneeda so easily. She focused her intention on finding Ivanna next. She knew it would take a while for all of her spells to work completely, so time was of the essence. "Ivanna will be an unsuspecting target, since she is always so busy entertaining her many guests."

Ivanna seemed ageless and could fit in with everyone no matter what his or her age or gender. Ivanna felt her own feelings with gusto but could also tell how others were feeling, which made her private gatherings that much more fun for everyone involved. Her immense capacity for pleasure brought highlights of joy and enthusiasm to the second floor of the crystal castle.

Fergetcha was jealous of Ivanna's warm personality and her easy ability to have so many healthy friendships. She knew that even though the grand festival brought great satisfaction to all the chakra sisters, Ivanna always wanted more of a good thing. Fergetcha plotted to lure Ivanna into her trap by inviting her to her own idea of a party.

Being a skilled shapeshifter, Fergetcha disguised herself with multicolored veils of thin gossamer, just the thing Ivanna would appreciate. She knew she could entice this sister with anything that was new, especially if it was soft, sparkly, or sexy.

Fergetcha knew that Ivanna walked to the lakes of Thisismeville each morning, and she was prepared to head her off track. Ivanna was up early this day, full of excitement and anticipation for what accolades might be forthcoming about the festival. She primped herself, changed into a half dozen different outfits, and waited for a longer time than usual for Aneeda to start the sisters' morning ritual climb to Iamone's meditation bed.

Being impetuous Ivanna, she became impatient. She figured her sister was just oversleeping because of the previous week's celebrations, so she headed out on her own this morning without waiting. Hoping to sneak a bonus cleansing splash from the fountains in the courtyard, she slid down the banister of the spiral staircase and ran through the front doors of the castle. Ivanna had no idea that her sister Aneeda was passed out on the first floor.

"Hello, Ivanna." Fergetcha moved quickly, catching Ivanna off guard the moment she stepped outside. "Your big party was quite a success, wasn't it?" said the Kundameanie trickster in the kindest voice, making no hint of her anger about not being invited. "Everyone in town is talking about how lovely you looked!"

"Oh, thank you!" replied Ivanna, always willing to receive a compliment. "Do I know you?" she asked as her eyes admired the many jewel-colored silken veils that covered the stranger's face.

"Not yet, but you will soon," chuckled Fergetcha to herself. Ivanna, being naturally amiable, didn't want to seem rude, but she couldn't figure out who this new visitor might be, so she invited her to speak more as she was drawn closer to the glistening threads.

"You like my beautiful garments, yes? I have more extraordinary shawls you might like to see, but they are in my new shop down the road. You really must come to feel them for yourself. The fabric is fabulous!"

Ivanna's ears perked up. "I don't recall a new shop in town! Have you been here long?"

"Oh yes, I've been around these parts for ages," said Fergetcha, "but I'm new to Thisismeville. Lovely little town," she lied. "By the way, I just hired some handsome handymen to help me out with the shop shelving. They were talking about you the other day and wanted to meet you."

"Special shawls, you say?" asked Ivanna enthusiastically, while picturing the handymen in her mind. Experiencing anything sensual was very natural for the second floor chakra sister who was at ease with herself and enjoyed making new friends . . . and shopping. She was more than willing to move toward another exciting adventure with this mysterious cloaked woman.

Fergetcha contemplated the web she was beginning to weave around the chakra sisters. "Follow me. My shawls come from the finest clothiers from many faraway and remarkable lands. You're going to love them."

Ivanna was caught.

Entering a small doorway, Ivanna marveled at the cozy shop that was filled with more colors, fragrances, textures, and glittering things than she had ever seen in one place. Quickly locking the door behind her, Fergetcha jumped on her chance.

"Here, Ivanna, breathe in this exotic oil. It will soothe all of your volatile emotions," said Fergetcha sweetly, while quickly waving a delicate bottle under Ivanna's nose.

"Volatile emotions?" thought Ivanna, "what a strange thing to say." She tried to ask the old woman her name, but the oil had an immediate intoxicating effect, both stimulating and sedating Ivanna's senses. Before she realized what was happening Ivanna was transported to a strange trance-like state of mind. She couldn't move.

Fergetcha began her tirade while Ivanna fell under the spell of the smell.

"I know what you're really like, miss fancy panties, bringing all of your boyfriends and girlfriends to your private den of pleasures on the second floor of the castle. I know how you secretly love to manipulate people, getting them to do whatever you want. You love the control, don't you, Ivanna? You want it all—the drinking, the drugging, the excessive appetite for food, sex, and fun. And you adore the adoration, don't you? That's all you live for, isn't it? You pleasure junkie, you!"

Ivanna's inner sensitivity caused her to feel the deep pain of this judging soliloquy, but she could not respond.

"I want this, I want that. I want, I want, I want!" mocked the sinister shrew as she flicked the shawls in Ivanna's emotionless face. "You always want more and more stuff! More relationships! More parties! More thrills! You can never get enough, can you, Ivanna? Face it, you're addicted to your endless desires!"

The creature paused for the slightest moment and said with a touch of sentimentality in her voice, "You have no idea what it feels like to really want something and not be able to have it. I've never felt happiness. I've had to sacrifice through all of my lifetimes. But you, little princess, are a spoiled rotten child, wanting all the good things in life while someone like me suffers endlessly. You are selfish and greedy!"

Fergetcha's voice was shrill again, but she knew she was getting through to Ivanna and aimed right for her gut. "You are the naughty girl in the castle with the risqué lingerie, and you love it! Shame on you, enjoying life with such wild abandon! You should feel *very guilty* for the way you behave, Ivanna. You and your sisters will surely suffer the consequences of your immoral choices."

By now, Ivanna was feeling the full effects of the potent poison that burned up her nose and into her brain. She was so confused by Fergetcha's cruel words that she felt herself go numb. If Ivanna couldn't feel anything, then she would forget who she was. That was all Fergetcha wanted. She felt she had a good start to the castle's demise, and it was still early morning.

Putting her snarling lips up to Ivanna's ears, Fergetcha whispered loudly, making sure her spell would settle deep into Ivanna's memory. "I will take from you what I have never had, Ivanna. I was never allowed the pleasure of enjoying anything, so I will make sure you lose your precious passion, Miss little-slutty-princess-on-the-ugly-orange-second-floor of your high and mighty castle. May your clear waters turn to mud!"

The Kundameanie energy was boiling in Fergetcha's veins by now. Feeling intoxicated by her own evil power, Fergetcha gathered her strength. She knew it was time to move on to the other chakra sisters. She propped the rubbery second chakra sister up on her shoulder, and they staggered and swayed together as Ivanna dragged her numb feet behind her. As quickly as Fergetcha had opened the bottle of toxic oil, they were out the door of the little shop of illusions, and headed back down the road toward the castle.

"So much for your endless joy and fun, Ivanna. The party's over," said the resentful Fergetcha. "You'd beg for my pity when you wake up—too bad you won't even remember meeting me."

Worn out from holding up Ivanna's heavy body, the determined spellcaster stormed in through the front doors of the castle. "Now, if I can just—hoist her up—high enough . . ." grunted Fergetcha, "I can dump her sorry emotional body back in her room on the second floor." Fergetcha knew that once her spell had been cast into the sisters' subconscious minds with her seeds of forgetfulness, the sisters themselves would do the rest of the work to collapse the castle.

The golden staircase was blocked. Aneeda's dead weight body lay across the first step. Fergetcha was pleased to see that there could not be much activity moving up to enliven the castle without Aneeda's help.

Exhausted from carrying Ivanna, Fergetcha dumped her right there, making a two-chakra-sister heap on the floor.

22

The Spell of Self-Doubt—Ahafta's Fires Are Extinguished

Bright morning sunlight filled the third floor as Fergetcha Kundameanie made her way up to Ahafta's domain. She was feeling even more determined now, knowing she had to work quickly to tap into the unsuspecting sisters' subconscious minds. It was most unusual to have someone walking through the castle uninvited, and Fergetcha did not want to be seen.

Ahafta, being quite self-disciplined and responsible, woke up early to take care of some tasks that had been set aside during the week of the festival. Looking out her large windows at the inviting warmth of the sunshine, she resisted the temptation to put aside her responsibilities to run outside and play. She was the follow-through chakra sister and knew her work must come first. Sitting at her desk, Ahafta felt immense satisfaction about how well she had mastered all of her tasks in order to manifest the grand festival.

"There is so much to accomplish, so many choices every day to stay on track with living my destiny." Ahafta knew exactly what she was meant to do: strengthen her personal power so that all of her sisters could feel good about themselves too. Her sisters Aneeda and Ivanna were mainly concerned with the material world, and Ahafta was the sister who could help them evolve to a higher sense of self. She taught them to take healthy risks and assert themselves with confidence.

She was just thinking of going downstairs to give her sisters a visit before their morning meditation when she noticed a figure dressed like an electrician walking through her foyer. Ahafta's gut instinct tugged at her insides when she spoke to the intruder, "Hello? Did Useeme send for you? She's the one in charge of our main circuitry."

"I was told that things were overheating here on the third floor. We'll have to quickly pull out these solar panel wires and douse those fires immediately."

"What!?" Ahafta couldn't believe what she'd just heard. No one had ever suggested something so devastating to the third floor.

Before Ahafta could stand her ground, Fergetcha instantly swirled into a tornado, blowing out all of the candles and bonfires that kept Ahafta's energy going. With one wave of her hand, she covered all the windows floor to ceiling with a multitude of dark tarps. Ahafta tried to scream for her to stop but began to lose her power without the energy of the sunlight.

In the darkness, Ahafta heard her heartbeat quicken. Fergetcha was nearby, but she was invisible to Ahafta. Every part of Ahafta's consciousness wanted to lash out and her insides felt like a violent volcano was about to erupt. She had more fight in her than her two sisters on the floors below, but Fergetcha's dark intentions were stronger and they struck at her prey like lightning bolts.

"I'm not going to waste my time, so listen well, Ahafta. I am Fergetcha Kundameanie and I have come to take my power back. Just *who* do you think you are, being so hoity-toity up here in a crystal castle? This is my land and you don't belong here!"

Ahafta's inner fire blazed at Fergetcha's criticism. Boiling mad, she retorted, "I don't know who or what you are, but no one can take my power away!" The Kundameanie spell felt like a vice gripping Ahafta's solar plexus, squeezing the life of out her.

In her usual ruthless style, Fergetcha planted the deadly seeds of doubt into Ahafta's mind. "You are a failure in every way, Ahafta. I've been watching you, and you have no idea how to work in the real world. My Kundameanie ancestors were the only group around here who moved together in perfect codependent style. No one ever left the herd or had the courage to step out on their own. No one in my history was ever bold enough to exert his or her individuality. Just who do you think you are?" It was the second time she asked that question, and Ahafta was so dumbfounded she couldn't find the energy to speak up for herself.

"You think you can do everything all by yourself, don't you, miss independent princess? But you are just arrogant and conceited. My family of Kundameanie energy will control the destiny of this castle once you are gone, so all of your perseverance and discipline will be worthless!"

Ahafta's stomach was churning while an ulcer was burning. She tried with all her might to punch this fiendish brute in the face, but it was too dark to see where she was swinging, and she felt too weak to lift her fists. Fergetcha was taunting her, daring her to lose her esteemed control.

"Your boldness will get you nowhere, Ahafta. Let me remind you that I am the one who is now letting your outrageous ego out of its cage. I control you! You will never take away my power to gripe or complain anymore. I rule the immense power of the negative world. You are nothing but a weak coward. You are not good enough. And you never will be, no matter what you do!"

Sickened by her own rage and sense of helplessness, Ahafta threw up, spewing what little was left in her stomach. In the background she heard Fergetcha. "Gotcha, didn't I? Where's your courage now? Where's your self-control now, miss big shot princess? Face it, I am right and you are wrong. Looks like your shining lustrous gem has just turned very dull, Ahafta!"

Fergetcha's hideous laughter filled the third floor of the crystal castle as she disappeared into the darkness, leaving the shivering and chilled chakra sister huddled alone in the corner.

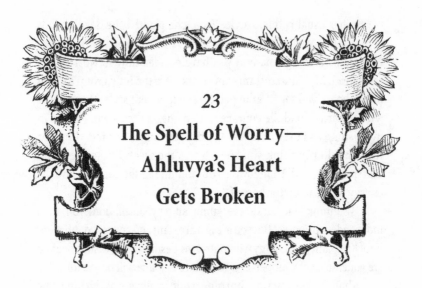

23
The Spell of Worry—
Ahluvya's Heart
Gets Broken

On the fourth floor, Ahluvya slowly woke up to her usual loving kinship and unity with everyone. This chakra sister was sensitive and her emotions were active, like Ivanna, except Ahluvya's love was even more expansive. Her vast heart space was inclusive to everything, which connected her to everyone's feelings in the castle and even beyond, into the surrounding lands of Thisismeville. Sometimes this gift overwhelmed Ahluvya when she sensed not only all the joy, but also all of the discord that transpired between people. This morning Ahluvya ignored the strange little tug in her chest and simply chalked it up to heartburn from the rich food at the festival.

Fergetcha knew that once she had weakened the chakra sisters on the first three floors of the castle the foundation would soon crack. She reveled in her ecstatic vision of the crystal castle crumbling away from the mountainside and crashing to earth in a storm of dust and broken dreams.

Paying a visit to Ahluvya was too good to pass up on this monumental day for the Kundameanie enemy of love. Pacing in her own internal misery, Fergetcha wanted her message of despair to tear through Ahluvya's heart in the most devastating way.

There was a sense of urgency here, because the electromagnetic energy was strongest on the fourth floor. It was not as visible or solid as Aneeda's, Ivanna's, or Ahafta's, nor was Ahluvya quite as vulnerable as her little sisters, so Fergetcha knew she had a tough battle ahead of her. Love was a foreign concept to the Kundameanie family, and Fergetcha had no idea how to get close to it. She kept her distance from Ahluvya.

Fergetcha's shapeshifting ability allowed her to hover outside the windows of the fourth floor like a clumsy bumblebee in flight. Here she could see everything without getting too close. She spied on Ahluvya at a coward's distance until her polluted aura caused the windows to fog up and become smeared with a slimy film.

Having no idea that Fergetcha Kundameanie was so close, Ahluvya slipped out of her bed and stopped for a brief moment to feel the soft green moss under her feet. She floated lightheartedly to her large windows, opening them to let the fresh morning air fill her floor.

It didn't take long for empathy to stir inside Ahluvya's heart. Her concern for everyone made Ahluvya the most beloved sister. This morning, she felt that something was going on in her surroundings, but she tried to focus instead on love and gratitude over the positive outcome of the festival.

"Her joy makes me sick," said the spellcaster to herself. "Nothing would make me happier than to smother all that caring compassion under a cloud of dark tension and stress! Now is my time to lock down that wide open heart of love of hers!"

Fergetcha created a vision of heavy chains, vaults, and steel doors covering over Ahluvya's heart, imagining the fourth chakra sister cowering in a prison of her fantasy.

Ahluvya could feel dissention and angst somewhere in the castle. It never occurred to Ahluvya that her sisters might be in jeopardy, but, come to think of it, they were getting behind schedule with their morning spiritual practices. Where were those girls anyway?

Ahluvya felt off balance with this fearful emotion rising within her. The very foundation of her castle was shaking! Aneeda, Ivanna, Ahafta! Her mind raced to her sisters on the bottom three floors and she knew something was amiss. Having no thought about herself or that she might also be in jeopardy, she only thought of her sisters. They were in grave danger and Ahluvya intuitively sensed that no amount of love from her could reach them now.

An acrid smell filled the fourth floor, and Ahluvya began to feel short of breath. Fergetcha was outside her window, gloating in her own self-importance. As Fergetcha's voice cackled, "I hate you. I hate you. I *hate* you, Ahluvya!" a new sensation ripped through the chakra sister. Apprehension! It gripped her legs, crept up into her stomach, radiated through her back, and landed right in her heart. It felt like an angry swarm of disturbed wasps had let loose inside of her chest.

"Ah ha! It's working already! I only have to think an evil intention toward her and it is hitting her smack dab in the middle of her smarmy heart with worry and anxiety."

Ahluvya's heart could not block out this dreaded feeling. Fear was beginning to cloud over the bright light that sustained her vibrant surroundings. The birds hid their little faces under their folded wings, and her garden songs became morbid and eerily still. Everything that Ahluvya had always felt with her loving heart was leaving her.

Fergetcha finally poked her head inside the fourth floor window now that her opponent had been weakened, and she shocked Ahluvya as she said, "I am having fun and I would love to see you suffer just a little bit more, but I'm sorry to say that I have to move on. However, here's one for the road, Ahluvya. The Kundameanie family decrees that your new energy of worry will cause inner conflict, fear, and loneliness to move into your heart, starting now!"

Like a deflating balloon zigzagging across the room, Ahluvya suddenly felt the life force drain out of her. A stabbing pain shot down her arms and back. She grabbed her pounding chest and fainted.

24

The Spell of
Dishonesty—Singya
Loses Her Voice

Fergetcha knew it was time to move upward to blot out the disturbing sounds coming from the fifth floor. With no energy coming up
from her sisters below her, Singya would be a cinch to capture. There
was very little protection around this small corridor of the castle.

Singya was singing as usual this morning, waiting for her sisters
to arrive, but it was getting late. With the lack of life-force moving
up to the fifth floor, Singya felt her voice becoming slightly hoarse
and her mantras sounding unusually coarse.

Fergetcha felt devious as her judging presence stepped onto
the fifth floor. She placed the tip of an ancient five-hole flute to
her cracked lips and began to play. The sweet sounds began to lure
Singya toward the spiral staircase.

The atmosphere was getting thinner the higher up the castle
floors she went, so every movement caused Fergetcha to gasp for a
deep breath. As Singya approached Fergetcha, she released the flute
and reached for Singya's throat with her deformed hands. With no
time to spare, Fergetcha wrapped an old bandana around Singya's

face before she could be seen and shoved a ball of thick socks into the mouth of the unsuspecting princess.

"Finally, you've been muffled! Your incessant squawking has kept the Kundameanie family on edge ever since you came to town."

Singya tried to cough, scream, shout, but Fergetcha was too strong for her.

"I am taking your voice away, Singya, so crying for help won't work. I have never been able to speak for myself. Besides, no one ever listened to me anyway. I have never been validated no matter what I tried to say. But now it's my turn!"

Singya squirmed under the tight grip of Fergetcha's gnarled fingers.

Fergetcha ignored Singya's gyrations and continued her rant, "Throughout existence, the Kundameanies have never been free to say what we wanted, much less sing or chant your hideous sounds. Any outward expression was slammed shut by my criticizing ancestors, unless it was gossip. Oh yes, we were very good at gossiping!"

By this time the fifth floor was wobbling and Singya felt her neck and shoulders tighten with pain. Her jaws locked up and she wished only that her hearing would stop long enough to block out the hateful voice blowing into her ears.

"You will never be free again, now that you have met Fergetcha Kundameanie. You will never again be able to trust what you hear as truth or lies! Oh yes, the Kundameanies are very good at lying, too!" Fergetcha was trying to catch her breath as she continued. "So, miss sing-along, you will no longer listen to your own intuition. You will listen to me now. And if you talk about me to anyone else in this unfortunate castle, no matter how hard you try, your sisters will not listen to you. They will accuse you of lying and no one will ever believe what you say again! In fact, from this point on even you won't be able to believe yourself! It's the ultimate Kundameanie way!"

Fergetcha was getting great pleasure from her own devious plot for the chakra sisters and continued to taunt Singya. "And here's the best part, you little irritating off-key princess. Of all your sisters, you will be the only one who will remember me. And not only will they not remember me, but they won't remember who you are, either!"

Singya's swollen throat felt like she had swallowed a cactus. She couldn't speak at all and stood blindfolded and mute while Fergetcha exited in a flash, causing a sonic boom to reverberate through the narrow fifth floor of the castle. Singya only heard these final grating words: "You'll never forget Fergetcha Kundameanie!"

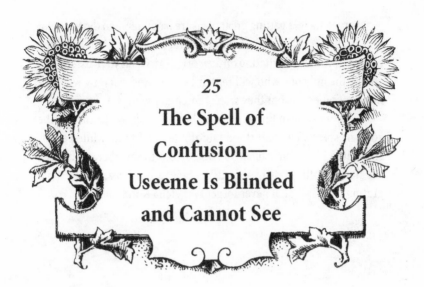

25
The Spell of Confusion—Useeme Is Blinded and Cannot See

When Fergetcha's blast erupted from fifth floor, Useeme was thrown back, landing with a thud on the floor. "What was *that?*" wondered Useeme out loud as the intense vibrations shook the precious vase holding her Flower of Insight.

Fergetcha was furiously bent on her mission now. She knew that the next two sisters would be the hardest to reach, and the formidable old conjurer congratulated herself for not having been seen by the all-seeing sister, Useeme, so far.

"Soon," thought Fergetcha, "Useeme won't be able to see any of her la-de-da visions anymore."

Useeme was quietly waiting in her meditation room for her sisters to come up and partake of the visionary elixir in the Insight Chamber when the walls began to rumble from Fergetcha's invasive blast of Kundameanie energy.

As much as Useeme was usually on top of things, this morning she was unaware while she allowed herself to indulge in some rare down time from the afterglow of the festival. Fergetcha was moving so quickly it was hard for the sisters to register the immediate effects of the spells that were being cast.

Before Useeme could reach for her precious vase Fergetcha had made her way into the center chamber between the two wings of the sixth floor. Just as she had snuffed out the fires on the third floor, Fergetcha immediately slipped a virus into Useeme's main computer and all the multicolored lights flickered off.

Useeme's clairvoyance allowed her to see apparitions on the sixth floor, so it wasn't unusual to for her to see a strange figure, whether they were ghosts or angelic beings. But this one was moving so fast she couldn't make out its true form.

With Kundameanie energy running amuck on the sixth floor, Useeme was completely disoriented. Fergetcha ran through the libraries in the west wing, tossing over file cabinets and destroying Useeme's books, records, and written discoveries. She then raced through the east wing with a laser beam sword, disrupting Useeme's intuitive equilibrium by smashing her art supplies and easels and ripping up her imaginative projects. The creative energy on the sixth floor came to an abrupt halt.

"Useeme, you've been hit with Kundameanie confusion, but let's be clear about one thing. I am Fergetcha Kundameanie, and I know you have never imagined someone like me before!"

Useeme couldn't see where this strange voice was coming from. Fergetcha continued, "Your little sisters already know me, so I will let you in on my story. I was never able to see any alternatives to the miserable life I have always had. My Kundameanie family has been stuck in a vicious cycle of fear and suffering for eons with no way out. We have been told that we live by a lesser mind because we cannot imagine any other way to live. But that is a lie. You are the one who is delusional, miss you-see-saw. To put it simply, you're time is over and my tribe is moving back into the mind of Mt. You'velostitnow."

Fergetcha's shapeshifting tricks made it more and more difficult for the chakra princess to perceive the truth of what was happening. Her eyes blurred with hallucinations. Without being able to see clearly, Useeme lost her ability to discern what was real from what was an illusion.

Then Fergetcha sped toward the final destruction on Useeme's floor: she broke the vase which held the sacred secretions of visionary power from the Flower of Insight. Useeme's formerly beautiful visions were flashing now as violent scenes of war and global decimation as Fergetcha projected her morbid innermost thoughts into Useeme's mind. She saw pictures of people, animals, plants, and planets in unbearable pain. Even though Useeme had once thought that she could have imagined all possibilities from every perspective, these scenes were completely out of her realm of rational and royal understanding.

Useeme had lost all logic, and her intuitive abilities fell silent. Her inner senses could only decipher that a very dangerous bomb had just exploded on her floor, shattering her life into pieces. She was left dazed and confused with a blinding headache and no memory of her sisters at all.

26
The Spell of Boredom—
Iamone's Lights
Go Out

The sun was rising a bit higher by now as Fergetcha hurried upward, forging ahead with her plan. Things were happening so quickly Iamone hadn't had a chance to process any of the new Kundameanie energies that were rising up through the crystal castle toward her floor. She was still feeling the joy of the festivities as she awoke this morning. High atop her lotus bed, she watched a thousand stars above her slowly fade away into the light of a new day.

Fergetcha was getting weary. She was almost out of her own energy. It was not part of the Kundameanie's modus operandi to use anything other than their ego's will and force to get through life. That made things quite exhausting, which is why they had challenging health issues from generation to generation. They fought and resisted any kind of impulse from a universal essence because they thought their low vibrations were all that existed.

The spiritual emanations from Iamone's top floor intimidated Fergetcha the most. She was unfamiliar with the pure sense of unity that vibrated here. The Kundameanie family raised Fergetcha to feel alone and disconnected from everyone else, but it was all they knew and they refused to change their old familiar ways. Any kind of spiritual practice for the Kundameanies was completely out of the question, and it was beyond their capacity to understand an enlightened state of being.

Fergetcha was losing steam. How could she break through the high energy that buzzed through her head way up here? She was also short of breath. She had never been in such a sacred place, and this frightened her more than anything.

Pulling out all the dirty tricks in her bag of disguises, Fergetcha paused for the first time. She had thought to transform herself into a bright star to attract Iamone, but emitting any kind of luminosity like that troubled her Kundameanie mind. She had no idea how to radiate light like Iamone could, and she could not imagine a disguise that could penetrate Iamone's high level of consciousness, but she was determined to finish the spell-casting.

Iamone was way ahead of Fergetcha's sluggish approach. By now she was aware that the castle no longer felt secure. Iamone could have easily floated beyond the castle's unsteady structure, but the thought of her sisters below changed her entire focus.

She assessed the situation in the castle, seeing it in her mind's eye. She saw Aneeda lying down on the ground floor. She could smell the toxicity of burning oil and charred wood coming up from Ivanna and Ahafta's floors. She began to worry and paced back and forth over her purple shag carpet. Her heart felt cold, and she noticed the eerie silence from Ahluvya and Singya's floors. There was no laughter coming up the spiral staircase, no sounds of pattering feet from her beloved sisters. Useeme's wisdom could not be felt, and Iamone began to imagine a frightening scenario.

At this point Fergetcha had turned her thoughts to her archaic Kundameanie training of separation, fragmentation, and divisiveness. She was thrilled with her own mission of severing Iamone's sense of unity and oneness. Once Iamone's thoughts turned downward toward her chakra sisters below, questioning what was happening in the castle, Fergetcha seized the opportunity. In Iamone's moment of disconnecting from the upper realms for just one split second of worry, the demoniac Kundameanie beast flew up and out the rooftop, slamming the skylights shut tight.

"Gotcha!" Fergetcha exclaimed with incredible exuberance. "All I needed was for you to be distracted, miss phony iamoney, to pull your focus away from your silly spirituality just the tiniest bit. You looked down, not up! Ha! Now, without your divine connection to your sisters and your celestial family, you will lose your worthless power and the kingdom will be mine again. You will have no purpose, no joy, nothing to do, and no reason to live. Your existence will be nothing but bland and boring, just the way the Kundameanies like things to be."

Fergetcha Kundameanie could feel her ancestors cheering her triumphant feat. "I won! I won! I won, Iamone! There will never be another spark of higher thought in your castle again. You and your sisters will be under my spell for eternity!"

Shrill, discordant laughter rattled though the late morning sky as Fergetcha quickly vanished over Mt. Iknowmenow. Stunned, Iamone dropped to her knees and held her head, feeling as though she had just undergone a psychic lobotomy.

27
The Spells Take Hold—
The 7 Chakra Sisters
Forget Their Natural
State of Being

Fergetcha Kundameanie's appearance had short-circuited the normally vibrant life force in the royal domain. Her essence remained in the castle for one full cycle of the sun and moon after the grand festival, giving Fergetcha's deceptive seeds of forgetfulness enough time to germinate inside the seven chakra sisters.

As the golden sun reached higher in the sky, the silent crystal castle appeared dull and colorless. The energy that used to bring liveliness to Mt. Iknowmenow was weakened by Fergetcha's spells. This new stillness did not have the meditative qualities that brought the usual peace but instead laid a painfully dormant feeling of emptiness on each darkened floor.

Life around Mt. Iknowmenow moved in slow motion as the turning wheel of the sun descended toward the horizon for the night. The townspeople of Thisismeville fought throbbing headaches from a thick pressure in the air. Their memory of the good festival was fading. Birds stopped chirping for their evening meals and sat like frozen snowballs on naked branches. The frogs stopped croaking, becoming miniature statues in the garden's pools. Neighborhood dogs wandered around, lost in the approaching dusk, and the fireflies drooped their little bottoms on the ground until their sparkles faded out. Even the moon had lost its reflective light and could not shine into the dusty windows of the castle. Fergetcha's spell had spilled over the land, just as she planned, turning Thisismeville into a ghost town.

∾

At the next sunrise after Fergetcha's violent rampage through the castle, before Aneeda could open her eyes, the ground floor chakra sister mentally scanned through her body, trying to bring some sense of physicality back to her awareness.

"Hey, Ivanna, get off me!" she shouted as she tried to shove her sister's dead weight off to the side.

"Huh . . . wha? . . . what?" Aneeda's scream was a shrill alarm to Ivanna, who was also struggling to get her mind connected back to her body.

"Ouch, stop it, Aneeda. You're elbow is breaking my back!"

"Moooove! Get . . . *off* . . . me, Ivanna. You're killing me!"

"Get your big, fat foot off my stomach!"

Aneeda and Ivanna shoved, punched, and finally managed to untangle themselves. They sat up and stared at each other sitting on the red rug near the staircase of the first floor.

"What the hell are you doing here?" sneered Aneeda.

"*Me?* What are *you* doing here?" Ivanna shot back. Neither one of them had an answer.

They looked around the first floor. Aneeda barely recognized anything, and Ivanna felt totally lost. They sat this way for a very long time. Neither one of them could muster up the energy to get up off of the floor so they just remained there, squinting incredulously at one another.

The spell was working right on schedule. Aneeda finally asked the stranger across from her, "Who are you?"

Ivanna felt a pang of sadness. She was at a loss for how to answer that question, then she doubled over with cramps, not saying another word.

Aneeda pushed herself up onto her wobbly legs. Turning away and ignoring the strange person on the floor, she did a zombie walk through the first floor until she found a refrigerator and stared inside. There was nothing there that resembled real food, but she was so hungry! And Aneeda couldn't remember what she liked to eat anyway.

Fergetcha hadn't missed a trick. She had filled Aneeda's fueling station the way her old Kundameanie family habits had trained her—with candy, chemical-laden diet soda drinks, chips, hardened cookies, and cakes smeared thick with icing in bright artificial colors. There were slabs of dead animal meat and a chunk of lard that was slowly melting on the countertop. Aneeda grabbed some donuts first, mindlessly licking off the sugary glaze that stuck to the corners of her mouth. It was the first taste that Aneeda's life was about to change.

Back in the foyer of the ground floor, Ivanna felt her bloated belly protrude as she lifted her stiff body onto the staircase. Feeling highly emotional, she cried all the way up to her room on the second floor and dove into bed. Having no previous experience of melancholy, Ivanna pulled the covers way over her head and felt new waves of emotions deep in her gut that scared her. Ivanna sobbed until she felt sleep overtake her. In her dream, she jerked each time she heard a loud gavel pounding as she watched one large lone finger pointing in her face shouting, "Guilty! Guilty!"

On the third floor, Ahafta could smell charred wood all around her. Nothing appeared different, but she couldn't see much since all the windows were covered with Fergetcha's dark tarps. The third floor chakra princess felt a dreadful coldness in her room. The only thing that was hot was her burning indigestion. Ahafta rocked herself to ease her stomach spasms but couldn't find the energy to move much more than that. She, too, had forgotten all about the life she had once lived so vibrantly in the crystal castle.

Ahafta felt too dead exhausted to do anything, and with no sense of motivation on this morning she just stretched out on her yellow couch and turned on the television. Lethargy sat down right beside Ahafta, like an annoying rash that wouldn't leave her side.

On the fourth floor, Ahluvya sputtered and coughed when she finally sat up on the side of her bed. It was hard for her to catch her breath and her heart was aching. She felt a tugging sensation in the center of her chest that wanted to pull her downward and upward at the same time, splitting her apart in the middle.

Forgetting all about their morning meditation ritual, Ahluvya knew that something wasn't quite right. She had never known worry before, but a cloud of anxiety was looming over her breaking heart. She felt alone, not remembering that she had six sisters who were in great need of her loving energy. Ahluvya stared at the yellowing green vines over her bed curling in at the edges. She felt the rough, dry moss poking the soles of her feet, amplifying her sense of dread.

Ahluvya's painful and sad heart sent the energy of loneliness up the spiral staircase to the fifth floor, where Singya was gargling to relieve her sore throat. There were no words, no songs, no creative buzz to be found anywhere in the small blue sound chamber, only a pure, throbbing silence that pulsed deep into Singya's ear canals.

"Please let there be an annoying cricket, the rush of a car driving by with a way-too-loud booming bass, a rustle of leaves, the sound of *anything!*" thought Singya. "I must be the only living thing in Thisismeville. I hear no sounds, no radio playing, no phones ringing, no little fingers tapping out a text message. Oh, to hear the beep of a construction truck backing up . . . even a hideous news station with babbling political discourse—I'd even be grateful for that noise. Just to be able to hear something, *anything* besides the sound of that cackling voice in my head!"

Singya covered her tender ears with shaking hands. She cleared her throat until it felt raw, and hummed a mournful dirge in her mind since no sound could be coaxed from her own mouth.

Useeme never realized that she had missed an entire day of castle activity. She woke up with a splitting headache and couldn't see anything. Everything was blurry, even in her dream state. Not only was her vision not functioning properly, but her memory was also failing. Useeme couldn't seem to recall anything of importance, but she had a vague nagging sense of having apocalyptic dreams. Within her dream world Useeme's mind created scenes that depicted her sisters' turmoil, although she didn't know it was from Fergetcha's spell. She struggled and tossed inside storm clouds, dodging boulders and sharp picket fences. Flooding downpours of rain morphed into tornadoes of fire, crashing through her windows and tearing her books to shreds. She heard ear-splitting sirens while sculptures of headless figures spun around her. Useeme saw disturbance in the castle but lost her ability to decipher any meaning from her vivid dreams. Little did she know that her sisters were also having warped visions and nightmares.

She couldn't remember how to maneuver her way through the sixth floor and found herself on the spiral staircase aimlessly winding her way up to Iamone's floor.

On the seventh floor, Useeme squinted into the darkness. Iamone was wandering around in circles, as disoriented as her sister. Unaware of each other, they mumbled and fumbled.

"Whazzat?"

"Who'sere?"

"Ge' away from me!"

"Where am I?"

"Whazgoin' on?"

Not recognizing one another, and each just as paranoid as the other, they circled around the lotus patterned carpet with their arms outstretched, fumbling around in the darkness. Suddenly, four hands landed on four shoulders as they merged arms length apart.

Wobbling on unsteady bodies, they faced each other, snorting like two bulls with horns locked.

They circled. Neither of them could break free. They were stuck in a repetitive pattern, going nowhere. The more they looked into each other's blurry eyes, the dizzier they became.

Frustrated, the two chakra sisters kept circling around and around, clasping on to the other's shoulders until they had wiggled themselves to the spiral staircase.

The other chakra sisters on the six floors below heard the tussle and managed to find their way to the staircase on their own particular floors. Feeling alienated and totally out of sorts with their circling dance on the top floor of the castle, Useeme and Iamone crashed and clashed their foreheads together in one swift crack. Losing their shaky footing, they tumbled over one another down the stairs. As they crashed through each floor they absorbed the other sisters in their avalanche.

Words that had never been uttered in the castle before spewed from the sisters in a tumultuous discord. A massive entanglement of hair, flying bodies, and screams ensued as the jumbled lump of sisters fell head over heels all the way to the ground floor, where Aneeda stood innocently licking the last of some donut icing off her fingers.

Aneeda took the brunt of the impact. Finding herself on the bottom of another pile of bodies, she and her siblings laid in a motionless heap on the red carpet. Then the moaning began. Legs wrapped around arms and feet were wound over necks. The twisted wreck could barely move, try as the sisters might to unfurl themselves.

"Why does this keep happening to me?!" shouted Aneeda before the other girls chimed in.

"You're poking me in the eye!"

"Ouch, move your butt!"

"Get your foot out of my ear!"

"Owww! My stomach!"

"Hey, your knee is jabbing me in the ribs!"

"Get off my head!"

"Quit pulling my hair!"

The longer they tugged to free themselves, the angrier they got. Finally, after a long bout of wrestling, each breathless and sore sister stood looking at the others with expressions of horror and disbelief.

Singya was the first to speak. "It was that awful woman! I forgot her name. . . . But she was here. Right here in our castle. *She* did this!"

"Our castle? What do you mean *our* castle? I'm the only one who lives here," said Aneeda.

"Not true, lady. I live here by myself," protested Ahafta. "Who are you?"

"Please, please, don't start yelling!" cried Ivanna, who was still reeling on an emotional roller coaster.

"*Listen* to me! I know what's going on here!" begged Singya, but no one was paying attention to her small, squeaky voice.

"I'm sorry to interrupt, but I really don't feel well," Ahluvya said. "I have a stabbing pain in my chest. Can someone help me, please?" She was trying to be polite but felt awkward amongst these strange people. It would be the last time she reached out for help from anyone.

"Well, that's too bad," said Ahafta sarcastically. "I'm hurting too, ya know."

"Sisters, *please.*" Singya tried again, but she was quickly interrupted by the others all at once.

"*Sisters?!*"

"Who are *you?*"

"I don't know you . . . "

"Who do you think you are?"

The barrage toward Singya seemed endless.

Ahafta felt a stabbing in her stomach when she heard the words "Who do you think you are?" She couldn't figure out why she felt so shaken about that, with all of the other commotion going on.

After her many spells, Fergetcha had the ability to listen to the sisters' thoughts. So, eavesdropping from a distance, she turned up the volume to hear what they said in their heads, making herself an invisible witness to their impossible situation. Clapping her hands together like a bratty little child waiting to unwrap a special gift, she relished the downfall of their energy.

Useeme was trying hard to make sense of all of this but could see that this was going to be an endless road to nowhere. Iamone was detached from the whole scene.

"OK," said Useeme, shaking some amount of cohesive thought back into her head. "I can see that we are all confused about what is going on here. I think I know how we might handle this." But Ahafta flashed back as she imagined her personal power being threatened, "Oh yeah? Who made *you* the boss, huh?" This outburst caused Useeme to shut down; it was the last time she offered her thoughts on anything. The scene repeated itself over and over with no one willing to budge.

Aneeda was only concerned about eating and was afraid there wouldn't be enough food if these other people hung around her floor. Ivanna was feeling emotionally drained and just wanted to avoid everyone and climb back under her covers. Ahafta, feeling self-conscious, vacillated between having no energy at all and aggressively blaming everyone else for this mess. Ahluvya's heart was breaking, and she felt alone and scared in this big castle with all of these upset people around her. Singya was getting more and more frustrated for not being heard and felt like she couldn't speak up or explain herself to anyone. Useeme kept getting distracted and couldn't concentrate on anything that was being said. Iamone found all of this nonsense boring and was apathetic to everyone else's problems.

Fergetcha Kundameanie was practically drooling with ecstasy. There was chaos in the castle, and Mt. Iknowmenow was rumbling.

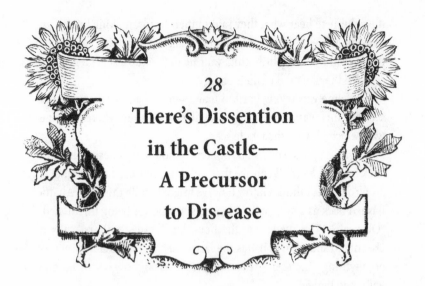

28

There's Dissention in the Castle— A Precursor to Dis-ease

"Can't anyone else hear that grumbling noise?" Singya was the only one to hear the deep rumbling in the bowels of the castle sounding like a gas bubble rolling toward eruption.

With no response from her sisters, Singya stomped back to her floor and started pounding on her drums. She was getting desperate for some attention. Opening her mouth wide, she howled out a long, frustrating scream. "Heelllllp! Somebody help us! Our castle is in danger!"

"What's that racket?"

"Finally," thought Singya. "I'm finally being heard."

She peaked out her door on the fifth floor to see her sisters standing there, looking annoyed.

"For one last time, I'm begging you to listen to me, please! We really are sisters, don't you remember? You have to hear what I am going to say."

"I don't havta hear nothin' you have to say," said Ahafta, wearing a large chip of arrogance on her shoulder.

Singya ignored the confrontation and continued, "It was that woman. . . . She attacked me! She took away my songs and my silences . . . and she took away everything from *you*, too!"

"What are you talking about? There was no woman."

"Yes! I'm telling you the truth!"

"Oh yeah? Then what did she look like?"

"I don't know. I never got a chance to see her. She blindfolded and choked me."

"Suuuure she did."

"And tied you up too, I suppose?"

"Yes, that too! She was very wicked. I could only hear her voice and smell her foul breath."

"Sounds like you were hallucinating."

"Maybe it was just your own foul breath you were smelling."

The sisters continued to taunt Singya, which infuriated the fifth chakra princess. She wasn't able to get her point across or put her words together in any effective way. She was losing her ability to communicate with her beloved family.

"It *was* that woman. You *have to* believe me!"

"You're lying! There is no woman."

"No, it's all true . . . her hands . . . and the boom. . . . Didn't you hear it? . . . So loud . . . then, the silence . . . then my ears exploded."

Useeme flinched as she remembered something about an explosion, but nothing was clear in her mind.

"This girl is delusional. What is she doing here, anyway?"

"Why should we believe you?"

"Yeah, you don't know anything!"

The sisters stood with their arms folded over their midlines in defiance of Singya. They looked like a stone wall that could not be penetrated. Truth or no truth, they wanted nothing to do with Singya.

"But you don't understand! It was—she grabbed—I mean, there were dark . . . I started to . . . I mean, I tried . . . and then she . . ." Singya couldn't find the words and continued to stumble over her tongue.

"You're not making any sense. I've had enough of your stories."

"Me too. I'm outta here."

"But I'm Singya, your sister!"

"You're lying!" they all screamed at once.

"Please listen to me!"

"No one wants to hear what you have to say, singsong ding-dong, or whatever your name is."

"And you're *not* my sister!"

This outburst hurt all of the sisters and they pulled back a little, but no one would ever admit that they felt Singya's discomfort. It was the beginning of a long string of mistruths and lies that would haunt the castle for days to come.

29

Ahluvya Worries—
Separation Starts from
the Center Floor

After a long day of disagreements, the sisters, who had forgotten that they were actually sisters, finally departed from one another feeling insulted, hurt, abandoned, angry, and full of fear.

Ahluvya found her way back to the center floor of the castle. Worry tugged at her. She was still vaguely aware that there were people on the three floors below her and above her. She had once understood the sweet pull of the human heart from below and the pull of the divine heart from above. But now all that had changed.

Ahluvya felt no pull at all, not downward, not upward. There was a very weak pulse of electromagnetic energy on the fourth floor, and her heart continued to throb. She felt a deep sense of loss, and this made her want to withdraw from the world. Ahluvya ignored her songbirds, plopped down on her dying brown moss carpet, and sobbed.

Ahluvya had forgotten all about her sisters and had no reason to live without anyone around her to love. She had forgotten all about loving herself as well. Loneliness blew through the empty hole in her heart, as cold as the winter winds.

"I feel dizzy and woozy. I am out of balance. But why am I so disoriented? My hands ache. And what is this odd pain in my arms? Arthritis!? It feels small and cold in here. I better turn off those blowing fans," wheezed the sister of the heart. "They are not helping this incessant cough. Oh, I just wish I could breathe! I hate this congestion!"

Ahluvya was shocked at hearing herself say the word "hate." That vibration had never been felt on the fourth floor. The spell was working; she was forgetting who she was.

As her lonely pity party continued, Ahluvya started to worry about her health. She worried about her favorite pink rose petals that had turned grey, dried up, and now crunched under her feet when she walked. She worried about situations she didn't even know about. The details didn't matter, it just felt "wrong," and she spent endless time worrying over things in her imagination. All this worrying made her sad, and her sadness made her afraid.

It all started from the center. With Ahluvya's fateful state of depression, everyone else in the castle was affected. Her heart-strings were out of harmony, and Ahluvya did not know how to retune them. Without love, the sisters on the other floors could not make a connection to each other. Each chakra sister pulled away from the others and began to live all alone under Fergetcha's spells.

The castle lights dimmed and flickered often. The townspeople could not see the shine from within the windows, and this affected their everyday comings and goings. Depending on how the chakra sisters were behaving, the energy in the whole castle felt scattered and chaotic or dull and lackluster. One day, the whole town of Thisismeville felt a nervous breakdown coming on when they saw different floors of the castle display a disturbing light show, some lights glaring and other floors completely dark at the same time. There was emotional stress and great dis-ease on Mt. Iknowmenow.

30

Iamone Forgets Who She Is—There's a Dangerous Disconnect on the 7th Floor

On the seventh floor, Iamone's mind was racing and she couldn't stop pacing. It was nearly impossible for her brainwaves to enter the deep healing state of theta, which used to calm her brilliant mind. She could no longer meditate after her huge fall down the spiral staircase, and she often felt dizzy and lightheaded. Iamone's separation from her sisters on the floors below weakened her immune system, affecting her body, her mind, and the whole castle in ways she did not understand. Her sisters never came up to visit her on the top floor, nor did she go downstairs to communicate with them. Without the energy of her other chakra sisters, Iamone lost her imagination and her spiritually advanced dream states turned psychotic, which threw everyone into a tailspin.

Worst of all, Iamone forgot about her connection to the spiritual realm. She was lost without the daily download of energy from the Queenking. The universal wisdom from the vast cosmos couldn't reach Iamone if she wasn't reaching back to receive it, but she didn't seem to care. She had forgotten that there was a team of spiritual helpers eagerly waiting for her right outside her windows. No matter how hard the angelic realm might have tried to reach her, Iamone wasn't even aware of their presence. The violets that encircled her tall lotus bed had withered, and the thousand white butterflies that flapped outside her windows went unnoticed.

On the days when Iamone was bored with her own apathy, she turned toward the material world and tried to be intellectually superior to everyone else. Thinking that this would fulfill her in some way, she allowed an egotistic, small-minded, controlling energy to take over. It was a game that was foreign to Iamone, but the Kundameanie spell of forgetfulness had caused her own sense of the divine mystery to fade away, just as it caused all of the sisters to behave in ways that were the antithesis of their natural ease and perfection.

Eventually Iamone lost interest in this game, too. With her skylights locked down, she was closed off from the creative world of distant galaxies and the possibility of expanding her mind beyond the confines of her closed walls on the seventh floor.

31
Useeme Can't Make
a Decision—
Her Third Eye
Gets Blurry

With no lights coming from the top floor, Useeme walked right past her meditation chamber where the daily dose of sacred nectar from the Flower of Insight was wasted as it dripped on the floor and began to dry up, like Iamone's violets and Ahluvya's rose petals.

Useeme's intellect left with Fergetcha. Her dictionaries and books collected cobwebs and dust. Her computers crashed, papers piled up, and her once favorite documentaries bored her.

"Why bother to write or paint? I can't learn anything new. Besides, my vision is so blurry I can't even see my own imagination! I'm lost!" Useeme's third eye was going blind, closing down her intuitive senses. Without much planning or deliberate thought, Useeme became undisciplined and her floor turned chaotic.

"Who are all of these odd figures running around here? I must be hallucinating again. Go away and leave me alone! You're stressing me out and the anxiety is killing me!" Useeme, like her sisters, was talking to herself, but she was the only one who thought she had strange visitors on her floor who were talking back. She heard voices that said she should get her head examined, but Useeme ignored herself and locked the doors to both wings on the sixth floor, feeling a heaviness of paranoia cover her eyes.

Useeme did the very thing she had warned her sisters about before the spell: she fell asleep.

Fergetcha had played the mad scientist, and the sixth floor experiment turned horrific, blocking the whole castle's ability to think clearly. The lingering trauma held Useeme captive with confusion swirling in her head.

32

Singya Is Feeling Bad Vibes on the 5th Floor—"Why Won't They Listen?"

Meanwhile, Singya was still trying to make sense of what was happening to her and her sisters. She began to feel a desperate and overwhelming sense of responsibility to tell them about what she remembered but held back, fearing that she might cause more pain and divisiveness. They refused to listen to her, and she had no one to talk to about the trauma that the castle was experiencing. The stress was causing her to grind her teeth, which made her jaw feel tight and heavy. Her tonsils and thyroid were swollen, and her constant sore throats infected her ears.

Over time, the fifth floor squeezed and wheezed inconsistently with either too much or not enough energy to cause the voice strings of her instrument to be played well. Some days, there was so little energy circulating in her sound chamber that she withdrew and became sadly introverted, too weak and shy to speak at all. She tried to write a letter, but the words wouldn't come. Frustrated, Singya threw her journals away, tore up her poetry books, ripped apart her wind chimes, and smashed her drums.

She was tormented by a sharp pain in her neck and the sound of "Fergetcha Kundameanie" rolling inside her head. The more she thought about the Kundameanie prophecy, the more troubled and hopeless she felt. Instead of being honest and standing up for herself, Singya rebelled by becoming loud and boisterous. She knew she was lying to herself. She began to speak with anger and sarcasm in her voice. Nothing was pure on Singya's floor anymore. Feeling out of harmony and lost without the love from Ahluvya, her discordant discourse with her sisters caused Singya's teeth to rot. This unhealthy state of dis-ease made all the sisters argue, judge, and criticize each other. Singya's harsh words shattered the windows of the castle and her lost soul just wanted to escape through the cracked glass.

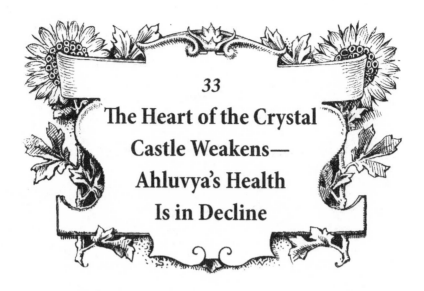

33
The Heart of the Crystal Castle Weakens— Ahluvya's Health Is in Decline

On the fourth floor, Ahluvya was so out of balance that she vacillated between avoiding all relationships and desperately clinging to others. No loving energy was coming from above to nourish her spiritual longings and no energy was coming from below for Ahluvya to establish her loving presence on the earth plane.

Ahluvya's self-imposed isolation translated into unhealthy cardiovascular problems and respiratory ailments. "I have issues in my tissues, my heart is offbeat, I can't take a deep breath, and my breasts are getting lumpy. I have a hideous skin rash, too. I don't want anyone to see me this way!"

Chronic pain settled into her upper back, her shoulders locked up, and her arthritis worsened as she stopped reaching out to the world. Ahluvya had completely forgotten that she had sisters whom she once loved so much. The heartbreaking loneliness caused her chest to cave inward, which in turn made the castle begin to buckle.

34
There's Trouble on the 3rd Floor— Ahafta Becomes Compulsive

With the weight of a slowly crunching castle above her, Ahafta on the third floor sensed an impending danger. Fergetcha's spell caused Ahafta to doubt herself in every moment. Looking in the mirror, her reflection scowled back with the face of a menacing judge who threatened her with a lifetime of punishment because she broke some unknowable rule or didn't do something exactly right. She wanted to blame someone else for making the wrong choices for her, to defend herself, but she didn't know why.

She lugged herself around the third floor, holding her stomach. It was hard for her to digest criticism, especially from her mean inner judge. She didn't want to swallow or internalize anyone else's opinions or thoughts either, and it was hard for her to maintain her own sense of herself.

The third floor of the castle started to ooze a green bile-like substance from the walls. Feeling disempowered, rejected and bitter, Ahafta was incubating diabetes, pancreatic problems, liver disorders, and gallstones. Her internal suffering caused the solar panels to fall apart on the third floor, sapping the energy needed to run the castle.

As Ahafta lost her confidence and personal power, she tried to make up for her low self-esteem by dominating others and pushing herself to be extremely competent. She used her ego's perfectionist willpower to exert the fire in her belly. Fergetcha's spell tore into Ahafta's stomach while her mind ran in endless circles, commanding her to "work, make money, consume . . . work, make money, consume . . . Work! Make Money! Consume!"

"Ahaftagetitdone. Ahaftakeepgoing. Ahaftaprovemyselftoyou."

Without having purpose or self-love from her sisters, Ahafta compulsively drove herself to maximum stress levels and her robotic life wore her out.

Ahafta was the sister who had always gotten things moving in the castle, but now she felt overwhelmed by running on a treadmill of meaningless action. "There are just too many webinars, seminars, telesummits, blogs, tweets, meet-up groups, magazines to organize, books to read, emails to write, calls to make, bill collectors to pay, and papers to file," whined Ahafta. "With all this information pouring through the airwaves so quickly it is impossible to keep up! I'm sick of feeling so stressed out and responsible for everything. I quit!"

Ahafta's procrastination eventually led her back to her yellow leather couch, where she plopped down and consumed bag after bag of potato chips.

35

The Castle Slips and Slides—Ivanna Forgets How to Go with the Flow

After Fergetcha's visit, the sisters' connection to the sixth floor circuitry was severed. With no program to receive and process how the sisters were feeling, everyone's negative and fearful emotions were suppressed, depressed, and impressed on Ivanna's second floor. Under this onslaught Ivanna was at the mercy of her own unbridled desires and raw emotions.

"Ivannafeelgood. Ivannanewdress. Ivannanewcar. Ivannanewboyfriend. Ivannalotofmoney, Ivannamanipulateyou, Ivannahavesex, Ivannalotofpower, Ivannabeabundant. Ivannaownyou. Ivannagoshopping. Ivannahavesomeonepayattentiontome. Ivanna. Ivanna. Ivanna."

Fergetcha caused so much confusion in Ivanna's energy field that the chakra sister on the second floor had forgotten how to go with the flow. She was torn between wanting to be social and wanting to be a recluse. The emotionally sensitive chakra sister ran so hot and cold that her natural yin and yang blurred and melted together, dissolving her unique ability to appreciate differences. She no longer found pleasure in duality or anything that was outside her comfort zone.

Feeling too much, too deeply, and too often made Ivanna want to turn all of it off. She became frustrated when her incessant wants for self-gratification were not immediately fulfilled.

Forgetting her truth, yet still wanting to be acknowledged, Ivanna took out her journal and wrote her innermost feelings and thoughts. Confused and consumed by the Kundameanie energy that was flowing through her, she wasn't sure how to make friends or have meaningful relationships, so she made them up in her head.

I don't know who I am anymore. And who are you? I feel so manipulated by you, but I really want to have power over you. I've taken on all of your miserable moods. Are these my feelings or your feelings? Does that mean I am codependent?

I don't want you to know this, but I'm really jealous of you . . . and I hate you. You make me feel so bad . . . and sad. I'm depressed. But I want you to adore me—please love me!

Don't talk to me about sex! I'm too self-conscious! I'm embarrassed about having sexual desires. I must hide how I feel, and that makes me so angry! But I feel so guilty and ashamed that I really want some good sex!

I really want you to like me. OK, so I will give up my personal power to you. If I help you out and do what you say all the time, you might give me the approval I want so badly. I want to win your love, and if I don't get the love I seek, I will sacrifice the last of my own dignity in order to get it! You'll see . . . and then I'll suffer every day for the sacrifice of my martyred self. And you will certainly know all about my suffering and sacrificing!

I have women's issues now. I think I might be developing colitis. I have diarrhea, I'm bloated, and I always seem to have abdominal pain. I have shoved my anger down for so long that I have urinary tract problems and I think I might even be developing kidney disease. And my PMS is outrageous! Face it, I'm doomed! I'm sick of being sick, but I can't stop feeling pissed off about everything!

Like Fergetcha had planned, the second floor chakra sister was forgetting who she was as a vibrant, sensual, and creative being. With deadened senses, Ivanna lost her desire for food or anything that nourished her pleasure centers. She lost her joy of constructive creativity. Under the spell, the clear pools on the second floor turned stagnant, attracting bugs, mosquitoes, unhealthy relationships and other pesty people into Ivanna's life.

"These damn antidepressants aren't doing a thing for me, and I'm sick of trying to calm down. But I really don't want to feel what is trying to erupt inside of me. Pass me a joint, or another drink, or maybe just one more Valium so I can finally relax," she mumbled to herself. "Numb is so nice."

But Ivanna's moods were inconsistent, and she got bored with numbing herself. In an effort to wake up her feelings, she became wild and unpredictable, sometimes unleashing a fetid fury like a sewer pipe bursting after a torrential downpour.

"I might as well rev it up all the way!" said Ivanna recklessly, heading toward a cliff of overindulgence and obsessive attachments to stimulants. She started gambling, and her excessive lifestyle of frivolous consumption led to addictions of all kinds. "I want more sugar in my coffee! I want more candy! I want more thrills!"

Ivanna thought that if she could just acquire something new or different—a few more material things, or friends, or intimate relationships, or just one more cigarette or chunk of chocolate—she would feel better. But nothing helped. On one hand she felt guilty for wanting things without meaning; and on the other she felt guilty for negating her inner desires.

Eventually, Ivanna became fearful of change or movement of any kind, and this inflexibility made her body rigid and her sexuality frigid. She felt guilty for not being able to move forward gracefully. The second floor sister lost her ability to set healthy boundaries for herself and began to feel very guilty about everything she did or didn't do. She didn't realize that when Singya couldn't say yes or no with confidence, neither could any of the sisters.

Ivanna's vacillation between too much and too little resulted in endless tears and numbing, dry emptiness, which made the whole castle feel like a complete breakdown was on the horizon. The castle on Mt. Iknowmenow started slipping down a sloppy mudslide.

36
The Foundation Is
in Danger—Aneeda
Becomes Needy and
Loses Her Footing

Fergetcha had successfully planted the seeds of doubt deeply into the minds of each chakra sister. They had forgotten who they were. She gloated over how well her scheme was taking over within the castle walls.

None of the seven chakra sisters was aware that her own individual problems were affecting each of her sisters in the same way. Each problem piled on the others, exponentially reverberating up and down the spiral staircase. When Iamone on the seventh floor lost contact with her spiritual messengers, all the sisters became disconnected to their unified field. Useeme's loss of perspective meant that the sisters lost their ability to gain insight into their challenging situation. When Singya lost her voice on the fifth floor no one could speak the truth.

On the fourth floor, when Ahluvya forgot her ability to lovingly connect with the world, she contracted her heart into a selfish ball of fear and loneliness. The other sisters felt this deeply, some expressing themselves with anger or sadness, others with depression, withdrawing, or lashing out thoughtlessly. With no energy of love or joy circulating through the castle, each sister felt that life was not worth living. What was the point?

Moving down to the third floor of the castle, Ahafta's lack of integrity with her energy caused all the sisters to feel like they were having a breakdown. No one was able to digest anything of value, and the castle became toxic.

Without Ivanna's natural enthusiasm and appreciation of the sensual life on the second floor, her sisters felt self-conscious and guilty for just being themselves.

When the vicious cycle from Fergetcha's spells landed with blunt force on Aneeda, no one in the castle could feel safe or secure about anything. With no energy coming up from the ground floor, the health of the whole castle was in danger.

On the first floor, Aneeda wandered around looking for more food. She felt the heaviness of the castle weighing down on her, with the upper floors' energy of substance abuse, poor boundaries, overwork, laziness, loneliness, dishonesty, confusion, and lack of purpose. She was scared and felt alone. Without her connection to her sisters, Aneeda had no reason to live.

Aneeda paced, tugging on her hands. Worry was creeping up her legs and she felt weak and wobbly. Sitting down to catch her breath, she began to realize the magnitude of her dilemma. She had forgotten how self-reliant she used to be, trusting in life and knowing that she could take care of herself.

Without her sisters' energy to lift her dense energy up the spiral staircase Aneeda's only thoughts were on herself and how she would be able to survive without someone else to take care of her. She had lost her family, her tribe, her sense of belonging to a support system. She harbored irrational fears about getting her basic needs met. Did she have enough money, shelter, food, and belonging?

Feeling extreme deprivation, Aneeda accumulated a lot of stuff because she was afraid to let anything go. Her need to clutch to people for fear of losing them backfired, as no one came to visit Aneeda anymore. Holding on to things so tightly made Aneeda constipated.

She believed that she didn't matter at all, so she neglected her health and started to binge on junk food, forgetting all about her organic gardens. She filled herself with empty calories and became overweight just to feel that her body was still part of her and that she mattered by becoming more matter herself.

She lost her connection to nature, to her sisters, to the whole castle. She lost her courage to explore beyond the castle walls. Something in the back of her mind nagged at her about how unsafe it was to be in the woods, so she stayed home with her fearful thoughts and developed hemorrhoids and sciatic pain.

The ground floor chakra sister whined out loud as she huddled on her red bed, "No one will come to hold me or save me. No one is going to rescue me. Oh, poor me . . . no one likes me. I'm lost and alone. I'm missing something, but what?"

Rocking back and forth, Aneeda could find no comfort. "I'm so scared! Where is everybody? I need someone, but I don't trust people. It's not safe to be with anyone, but I need someone to tell me what to do. I can't take care of myself. What should I do now? I am helpless, it's no use. I can't do anything. I need a mommy!"

"Hey, wait a minute. . . . Do I have a mother? Do I know her? Where has she been? I've been abandoned!! How did I get here? How was I born!? Why was I born anyway? Aneedaknowwhoiam!"

Feeling fearful, Aneeda believed in the limitations of a big, cruel world. Because she felt like a victim, Aneeda became very needy.

"Aneedapproval. Aneedacceptance. Aneedanewbody. Aneedalotofattention. Aneedaeat! Aneedamotherwholovesme. Aneedamindofmyown,butwilldowhatyousayinstead . . ."

The crumbling foundation of the crystal castle was now precariously perched on the side of Mt. Iknowmenow. Everything was falling apart, and the energy needed to hold it together was dangerously low.

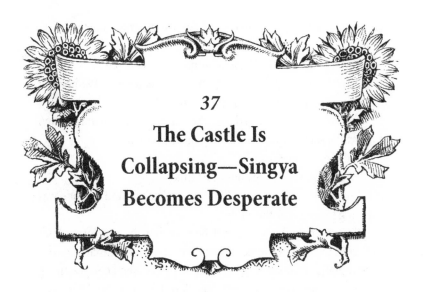

37

The Castle Is Collapsing—Singya Becomes Desperate

The woebegone chakra sisters wandered around their own floors of the sick castle. The spiral staircase was falling apart on the inside while the walls outside cracked and buckled. The castle lights had gone out and no one knew what was happening. Even the Queenking did not know the fate of their future. Without the sisters activating their natural energy the whole castle would collapse, signaling another timeless period of death and darkness on Mt. Iknowmenow.

Singya was the only one who seemed to vaguely recognize the other life forms in the castle, even though all her sisters had forgotten about her. Carefully, she maneuvered her way over the broken slats. No one went up or down the spiral staircase anymore because it was so insecure. The polished gold was now dull and scratched. Singya made her way down, ignoring part of the handrail that cracked off and clunked to the ground floor as she passed.

Shouting out loud to anyone who might hear in the castle, her words bounced around the open space of the empty place. "Listen to me. I need to—I want to—I have to tell you something. It's important!"

"We've been tricked! Hoodwinked! We've been hacked and hijacked! Look around you. . . . This place is a mess. We have all been bamboozled with a spell and we must break free!"

Singya's shouting caused the other sisters to turn their attention toward the ruckus that was echoing on the staircase.

"Oh no, not *her* again!"

"What's she blabbing about this time?"

Their apathetic voices faded into the background. No one was listening to Singya at this point.

Singya knew this would not be easy, but she was losing faith in herself and did not remember how to communicate clearly with pure intentions. Since Fergetcha's appearance, she kept practicing positive affirmations up on her fifth floor hoping it would awaken her sisters, but to no avail. She knew that without the energy of her sisters' wisdom, gratitude, love, and strong emotional charge behind her affirmations, they were just ineffective words repeating themselves over and over without any power.

The expressive princess didn't know which sister to reach first since they all had their own unique gifts that were needed for the castle to survive and thrive. Singya knew they had to function together as a team.

The banister was swaying, and Singya realized the foundation of the castle needed shoring up right away. Her mind raced to Aneeda as the staircase got shakier with each step. The farthest she could go was the floor beneath her, to Ahluvya. "Yes, *love*. We need Ahluvya's heart of love to get us moving again!" thought Singya.

Singya cautiously wound her way to the fourth floor where she saw her sister sitting alone among dried up ivy vines and shriveled kiwifruit, staring out the smear-stained window, looking at nothing. She barely looked up when Singya walked in. Singya approached her respectfully, trying hard to find the right words to say to this lonely and forlorn figure in the windowsill.

"Hello, Ahluvya. It's me, your sister Singya." No response.

"Ahluvya . . . Hey! Can you hear me?" No response.

"Don't you remember me?" prayed Singya with waning hope.

"She's barely breathing," thought Singya, getting more worried over the weak energy in the heart center of the castle. Ahluvya's isolation was causing her heart to skip beats, and her breathing slowed to just a shallow shadow of her former expansiveness. Singya shouted in Ahluvya's face, "Wake up, sister!" Still no sign of contact, which made Singya sink into a deep sadness.

They sat silently together but worlds apart. Singya had once loved her times of silence, but this was unbearable. Ahluvya had withdrawn into her own little self-centered place of fear and worry, neither reaching out to others nor receiving any love for herself. Her inner conflict was so painful that Ahluvya chose to avoid being in any kind of conflict in the outer world. She could no longer bring healing to any people or situations that called for her attention.

Far in the distance of the diminishing kingdom, there was a faint, shrill call.

"What's that sound? Ahluvya, can you hear that?" asked Singya.

Softly at first, then louder as it came closer to Ahluvya's dust-smudged window, they heard the little bird chirp thrice, "MeeWee. MeeWee. MeeWee."

No one but the chakra sister on the fourth floor was familiar with this strange invocation, which only called for Ahluvya to notice it.

"MeeWee. MeeWee. MeeWee." Again in a series of three, the rare, exotic bird called out to illicit a response. Singya was captivated by the summons of this creature outside Ahluvya's window.

"Sister, it's calling to you. Wake up! What does it mean? Can't you hear anything? *Ahluvya, listen!*"

Ahluvya could not rouse from her trance, and Singya became more and more frustrated. "We need your love, Ahluvya. The castle is in danger. Our sisters are dying, and only your energy will spark their desire to love themselves enough to snap out of this spell!"

The beautiful MeeWee bird was still chirping its strange call. Singya felt compassion for the little creature because she knew how disappointing it felt to be ignored. Not wanting to leave Ahluvya, but knowing she had to do something quickly to keep the castle from collapsing, Singya ran to the staircase to venture up two flights to see Useeme. Maybe she could reboot her computers to bring clear thinking and life back into the castle.

Meanwhile, the MeeWee bird continued to call out to Ahluvya, waiting patiently for her to remember.

༄

Singya was dismayed at how disorderly things looked on Useeme's sixth floor. She called for Useeme, only half expecting any acknowledgement from her.

"Useeme, can you see me? You remember me, don't you? I'm your sister, Singya. I speak, and you see, but now you need to listen to me!"

Useeme was confused by another stranger walking around her floor. Not being able to discern if Singya was real or just another hallucination, Useeme cautiously waited before answering.

"Useeme, we are under a terrible spell and you have to wake up! No one is thinking clearly. I can't reach Iamone or Ahluvya or any of our sisters. Our castle is in grave danger!" Singya's voice was weakening as laryngitis settled into her throat. "Help! Please help us, Useeme. We have to find a way out of this trap."

Useeme watched this pathetic figure frantically moving her mouth but she didn't hear any sound coming out. "I can't hear a word you are saying. You must be another figment of my imagination. Just go away. I'm tired and I have a headache."

Useeme turned and walked back into her dark room. Singya was shattered. She wanted to scream but she couldn't. She tried to communicate telepathically, but that didn't work either. Feeling dejected, neglected, and disrespected, the chakra sister of sound went back to the fifth floor and cried hard, without making a peep.

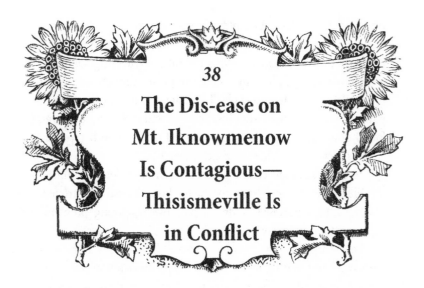

38
The Dis-ease on Mt. Iknowmenow Is Contagious— Thisismeville Is in Conflict

Every moment that ticked by, the ailing castle sank a little deeper down the side of Mt. Iknowmenow. The dis-ease of forgetfulness was eating away the life force on every floor like a menacing cancer.

The divine royal family had practically disappeared from Mt. Iknowmenow, and the townspeople were also feeling the negative effects of the Kundameanie spells. With the weakened energy of the castle, the spirit and goodwill of Thisismeville was dissolving. The entire community was adversely affected and everyone was suffering in some way.

It was a sad situation in Thisismeville. They had completely lost hope or faith in life's infinite possibilities. The townspeople, like the seven chakra princess sisters, had forgotten who they were.

The memory of the grand festival had faded long ago, and everyone forgot what happiness felt like. They were consumed with depressing thoughts and overwhelmed with conflicting viewpoints on the state of affairs in the village. Everyone lived in a constant state of lack, jealousy, worry, and anxiety. They judged everyone harshly, especially themselves. A deep divide was separating neighbor from neighbor, and almost everyone felt angry and sick most of the time.

Over time, the more they forgot about the soul's original promise of joy, a strange phenomenon of ego personality grew amongst the castle and the townspeople. Too many discordant thoughts of power, control, opinions, doubts, borders, and stubborn reasoning found dominance over the good potential that existed before Fergetcha's increasing divide and conquer spells.

In this dissonant conflict, vibrations slowed down in Thisismeville until everyone's heart contracted into a closed, constricted, disconnected emotional coldness, and overwhelming problems took over the whole town.

Fear was breeding greed in Thisismeville. There were riots in the streets and looting in the village shops. Corruption was rampant. People lied to one another and stole from their neighbors. Wars broke out. No one trusted himself or herself or anyone else.

Fergetcha Kundameanie's delight in their plight made her jump for joy. She was the master spoiler.

39
The Royal Parents Finally Wise Up— Don't Just Witness, Do Something!

Meanwhile, the omnipresent Queenking consciousness was watching everything from their floating penthouse over Mt. Iknowmenow. This high vantage point gave them an overarching view of the castle's hastening descent.

The Queenking knew all about the Kundameanie family and their outdated belief systems that revolved around fear, lack, and life-negating judgments. However, being the quintessential neutral observer, the Queenking never interfered with the free will of anyone in the kingdom. It was this natural gift of unconditional love that allowed everyone to learn and grow from their own choices, even if it meant momentarily forgetting their divine origins.

Once upon a time long ago, the lands around Mt. Iknowmenow had been consumed with warriors of ignorance. It was a dark time of wars, disagreements, and power struggles. People wasted their energy by trying to deceive, condemn, or suppress one another. The Queenking knew where and how Fergetcha was raised, and they felt compassion toward her. They knew her heart had been broken when the time of the Great Awakening in Thisismeville kicked the Kundameanies out of town.

However, the spells of forgetfulness were very powerful, and Fergetcha Kundameanie knew her craft well from eons of practice. Before the time of the crystal castle, every once in a while, she would visit her old stomping grounds around the mountain. She kept the townspeople asleep in darkness, which is why the Queenking had difficulty arousing them. It was only when the seven chakra princess sisters arrived that the light of awareness shone on Thisismeville, reminding the townspeople of their true origins.

Now the Queenking lamented, "We have failed our daughters by not making our connection stronger when they were young. With nonattachment and unconditional love, we gave them everything they needed. We trusted our precious daughters to mature on their own without our interference, but they were taken by surprise when the Kundameanie energy came back. We didn't want to alarm them with warnings of negativity, but we should have educated them more about the foibles of Fergetcha. Now it may be too late. They have forgotten their roots, forgotten all about the truth of who they are as family members in the Tribe of All-Knowing."

They concluded that Iamone must open her cathedral ceiling so cosmic spiritual nourishment could enter the castle once again, but the Queenking could not penetrate their daughter's sleeping consciousness. Nothing short of a gargantuan blast of spiritual energy would be able to shake the seven chakra sisters back into their natural harmony.

"We can hear Singya's silent cries for help." Even though the Queenking was the source of all the divine energy that animated the crystal castle and their seven daughters, Mother Queen and Father King knew it was time to summon more help. They called for cousin Oimalive Fundalini to bring her enlivening burst of life force. Aunt Ida and Uncle Pingala were notified about the broken spiral staircase. Signals were sent out into the vast cosmos. Spirit guides, angels, archangels, ascended masters, wisdom sages, alchemists, universal metaphysicians, extraterrestrial life forms, enlightened ones, and all evolved self-actualized universal beings of light were notified of the calamity on Mt. Iknowmenow.

40
Owl Woman
to the Rescue

When the call was sounded, the first to hear it was the old lovable Owl Woman. The ancient godmother stepped into the foyer on the first floor and felt the ground shake beneath her. With every step, it creaked and cracked a little more.

Owl Woman was shocked to see the overweight first chakra sister waddle out from the kitchen holding a fried chicken drumstick in one hand and a huge piece of chocolate cake in her other hand.

"Aneeda? Is that you? I hardly recognized you! What has happened here?" Owl Woman screeched, which scared the already frightened princess even more. Aneeda dropped her plate, splattering dark chocolate icing all over the red tiled floor. She tried to run away from Owl Woman but she was so out of shape she couldn't lift her swollen feet fast enough.

Knowing the danger that was facing the castle, Owl Woman flew to the second floor where she found Ivanna's favorite tawny pet looking like a scrawny alley cat dragged in from a fresh street fight.

The peaches on Ivanna's trees were dehydrated, and the once beautiful waterfalls had dried up.

The energy in the second-floor abode of the emotional princess was pulsing with heaviness and emptiness at the same time, like feeling too full and drained simultaneously. Owl Woman was concerned about this type of unhealthy duality.

"Ivanna, where is your joy? What happened to your spontaneous enthusiasm? Why has your juicy, fun life dried up!?" Ivanna was hiding under her covers and didn't bother to answer the call from the stranger in the hall.

By this time, Owl Woman was getting a clearer picture of the castle's grave situation as she flew up to see Ahafta on the third floor. An uncomfortable chill blew through Owl Woman. "Ahafta, there is no fire on your floor! There is no movement . . . it is so cold and still. What has happened to the power here?"

Ahafta was dwelling on her own thoughts of unworthiness and failure. She heard a voice but wasn't motivated enough to get off the couch.

Without waiting for an answer, Owl Woman felt the emptiness inside her own heart as she approached the fourth floor. "Ahluvya, most precious one, I am here!" But Ahluvya was so absorbed in her loneliness that she did not recognize love when it was right in front of her. Owl Woman could see the armor that was covering Ahluvya's heart and was most troubled by her blank stare. There was no possibility of connecting when the fourth chakra princess was so withdrawn into her own painful isolation.

Knowing she had to find the sisters on the upper floors, Owl Woman paid no attention to the disintegrating spiral staircase under her. Fly-running into the small round foyer on the fifth floor, knocking down more stairway slats in her wake, she found Singya. The once expressive princess was now rocking back and forth with her turquoise meditation pillow hugged close to her mouth.

"Singya, please tell me I am not too late! Can you hear me? It is me, your godmother, Owl Woman!" said the guardian, half shouting, and half pleading in a desperate but hopeful tone. Not only had

Fergetcha robbed Singya of her voice, but she had also blocked her ability to hear her own intuitive voice and the angelic messages. She was losing her gift of listening.

Singya looked up and thought she recognized an old friend from long ago, but nothing specific was coming to her. "What? Can you hear *me*?" asked the fifth floor sister, hopeful that someone might acknowledge the sound of her own lost voice.

"Ah, you can speak! How did our radiant castle get this way, Singya? It's practically destroyed!"

Singya hesitated, afraid to say anything. She assumed by now that no one would believe her anyway. "I don't know what is true anymore. . . . I can't remember."

Although Singya never actually mentioned Fergetcha's name, Owl Woman was beginning to understand, and she felt responsible for not better preparing the seven chakra sisters for what she now surmised must have happened to the castle's life force. The seven chakra sisters were not only asleep, they were in a deep stupor. Knowing this, Owl Woman's intuition was flashing on high alert. In all their travels throughout time, Owl Woman and Fergetcha had never met face-to-face. Fergetcha Kundameanie had always managed to fly below Owl Woman's radar, although the legend of the life-threatening Kundameanie energy always circulated around the wisdom keepers' conversations. Fergetcha's spells were renowned amongst those who had eventually woken up from the deep sleep of forgetfulness. Owl Woman felt the urgency to wake up the chakra sisters before the spell consumed them.

"Apparently, no one is talking to anyone . . . and you are the one who transmits and expresses all the messages in the castle! Singya," screeched Owl Woman, "answer me. This is important: can any of your sisters communicate with you!?"

Singya shrugged her shoulders, feeling the pain of past rejection from her sisters. "I can't say," she sighed.

Owl Woman was devastated, knowing that Useeme, upstairs, must have lost control of her energy from the main computer in the castle. Without Useeme's higher thoughts being transferred to the floors below, none of the sisters knew how to think, speak, or act with any clarity.

"Don't go anywhere, Singya. I'll be back!" Singya didn't say a word and kept rocking with her round pillow clutched to her throat as Owl Woman flew up to Useeme.

On the sixth floor, Owl Woman stepped cautiously over the books and art supplies that were scattered everywhere. Seeing Useeme for the first time, Owl Woman gasped, "Oh no, this is worse than I thought! Poor Useeme. She's lost her mind! Useeme, can you see me?" But Useeme couldn't see anything. Like Ahluvya, Useeme stared into empty space, not responding to Owl Woman.

It didn't take long for their beloved guardian to ascend to Iamone's room, anxiously anticipating her reunion with the precious, radiant, and wise chakra sister at the pinnacle of the castle. Although Owl Woman could see in the dark, Iamone's seventh floor seemed like the blackest illusion of all. Iamone's stringy white hair hung in her face, and she never acknowledged Owl Woman's presence. "Where is your light, Iamone? No one in the castle or Thisismeville can function without your spiritual light!"

The ancient medicine woman wasted no more time trying to awaken the seven chakra sisters. Without a sacred ceremony, there was no way she could break through the Kundameanie spells. Following her intuition without any doubt, Owl Woman spread her massive owl wing arms and extended her hands into colossal clawed graspers. She scooped up each chakra sister from the deteriorating castle floors and flew them in one large bundle toward the ceremonial field.

41

A Message
Is Revealed—
The Healing Begins

In the daylight, the seven chakra sisters could see the outline of the trees that surrounded the vast field. Their previous trips to this place had taken place under the stars, but they had since forgotten those nights of blessings and initiations. Now, they looked up into the expansive blue sky and felt the sun blasting life into them for the first time in a long while. Owl Woman knew that breathing in fresh air was the first step in their healing.

Before the sisters had a chance to fight, bite, or frighten one another, Owl Woman touched down in the center of the open field, placing them gently in a circle. They were surrounded by oversize red wildflowers, orange marigolds, towering sunflowers, green ferns, pink roses, blueberry bushes, indigo lilies, deep purple irises, and rows upon rows of lavender in full bloom. Owl Woman knew that if they could begin to enter the sensory world of colors, textures, and smells, they might feel their life force moving again.

The wise medicine woman had picked the location where the babbling brook ran through the field and the birdsongs accompanied the rustling wind through the distant treetops, hoping that the sisters could relax into the sounds of nature around them.

Struggling to keep the bright sunlight out of their eyes, they quickly shaded their faces. They were not used to being in this much light since the Kundameanie energy had taken over. They could barely see each other and didn't understand why they had been transported to this place.

"Lie down on Mother Earth," commanded Owl Woman, "and don't say a word!" Confused and traumatized from being bossed around, each distrustful sister hesitated in her own way. However, there was something about this majestic figure that seemed benevolent and familiar to the princess sisters, even though none of them could remember exactly how they might know her.

The sisters stalled, not knowing if they wanted to protest, but the whispering breeze felt like a warm massage through their knotted hair and the soft grasses under their bare feet invited them to obey without too much resistance.

Owl Woman lit dried leaves of white sage, which started their spiritual cleansing. She waved the smoke over the girls, clearing their energy fields with purity and intentions for a return to wholeness. Smell was a powerful sense, and this smudging was a wake-up call for everyone.

Aneeda's weight issues were affecting all of the sisters. None of them were feeling physically well because Aneeda had forgotten how to take care of her own health. It took a few moments for her to get enough energy to lower her large, heavy frame, but as her body finally unfolded on the ground, she heaved a huge sigh of relief.

Ivanna was still unsure of her relationship to these other strangers, and in spite of wanting to have an emotional outburst, she controlled her tantrum. This whole setup made her feel suspicious. When she felt everyone's eyes on her Ivanna became embarrassed, so she eased her stiff body down on a spot closest to the flowing stream.

Ahafta was more unsure of her relationship to herself than to these other characters, so she remained unmovable, taking a stubborn stance to hide her lack of self-confidence. Owl Woman stared straight into her eyes, which made Ahafta feel even more intimidated. Not wanting to be manipulated, she questioned whether she should listen to this strange command to lie down and shut up. Owl Woman didn't budge, so the skeptical third floor princess finally acquiesced, reluctantly. Lying on her back with her face to the full sun, finally soaking up the heat that she had missed for so long, Ahafta felt tears roll down to her ears.

Ahluvya was in a very weakened state when Owl Woman came to her fourth floor. But being outside under the open sky amongst all this life and greenery made her heart soften a bit behind its hardened shield. She took a rare slow, deep breath and let the beauty of earth hold her completely. Ahluvya rested there on the ground without moving, feeling the natural rhythm of her own pain-free heartbeat for the first time since Fergetcha's visit.

Singya wasn't speaking at all, like their guardian had ordered, although she still felt the urge to explain what she remembered from that fateful day of the spell-casting. Pausing from her frustration for a moment, she just listened instead. She heard the vibrations of the flowing waters, the flowers bending in the light winds, and the lulling sounds of the cicadas surrounding her. Singya laid on her stomach and heard herself quietly chanting *aauuhooommm* deep into the warm grass under her face.

Useeme seemed the most confused, being away from her familiar surroundings of computers and advanced thought forms up on her sixth floor. She did not have the gravitational pull that her other sisters had, and it was only through them that she could connect to the healing powers of the earth and her elements. She had forgotten all about that, however, until Owl Woman touched her forehead at the third eye. Owl Woman could sense her reluctance to make decisions and her inability to see anything clearly.

"It's alright, Useeme. Mother Earth is here to support us. Just relax and don't think about anything. Right now, the only choice you have to make is whether you want to lie down on your stomach or your back."

That seemed to take the pressure off and ease Useeme's indecisive mind a bit, so she lay down on her side, putting her left ear to the ground. Noticing this odd choice, Owl Woman knew that Useeme would need a lot of healing work during this sacred ceremony.

Lastly, it was Iamone's turn to follow the simple directions from the strange medicine woman. What was she supposed to do again? Owl Woman, being intuitively perceptive, heard Iamone's question and simply repeated, "Lie down on Mother Earth, Iamone, and don't say a word." Once Iamone made contact with the ground, it was the first time in a long time that spirit connected to earth for all the chakra sisters.

The seven chakra sisters stayed in this quiet position while the sun showered them with warm, comforting rays of light. They were simply being, listening to the sounds around them. They were not saying anything, doing anything, or arguing with each other outwardly, but inwardly their negative thoughts and self-doubts continued. Those abrasive inner voices were in direct conflict with the healing environment of nature where Owl Woman had brought them.

The birdsongs blended in harmony with the trickling waters. The faint call of "MeeWee, MeeWee, MeeWee" echoed through the distant treetops. The exotic MeeWee bird was coming closer, approaching the sisters with its high-pitched tune. Singya's ears perked up, being the intent listener. She sat up and looked at Ahluvya who was now also paying attention to this unusual friend.

The MeeWee bird landed right next to Ahluvya, boldly announcing itself. Ahluvya still could not figure out what the unique call meant and why this particular bird kept making a point to get her attention, but at least she was listening to it this time.

Owl Woman was watching this destined meeting, knowing that Ahluvya would need something extraordinary to shake her awake. The MeeWee bird danced around the sister of the heart, showing off its iridescent feathers "MeeWee! MeeWee! MeeWee!" Its hopping antics made Ahluvya laugh a little bit, a sound that was rarely heard anymore.

All the other sisters, except for Singya, were oblivious to the magnificent MeeWee bird and its showing off dance for Ahluvya.

Where had she heard this bird-chant before?

Owl Woman knew that she must not interfere with any of the chakra sisters' processes of awakening from Fergetcha Kundame-anie's spells. They had to do it on their own if it was to be a lasting healing. She said only one word out loud: "Remember."

"Remember . . . remember what? I can't remember what I am supposed to remember!" cried Ahluvya. By this time, Singya had moved to the opposite side of the dancing MeeWee bird so that it sat between them.

"MeeWee, Ahluvya. Remember? I'll try to help you find the words," said Singya, following Owl Woman's lead and gaining a little more strength in her voice. "Remember what 'MeeWee' means to you."

The brilliant MeeWee bird knew what to do. Hopping first in front of Singya, and then in front of Ahluvya, it went back and forth in a frantic dance, singing, "MeeWee! MeeWee! MeeWee!" Back to Singya with a sharp, single chirp, "Mee!" then to Ahluvya, with a crisp "Wee!" Three times it repeated this, bouncing from the fourth to the fifth chakra sister and back again.

"Go back, Ahluvya. Go back to the earliest memory that you have," said Singya, taking Owl Woman's hint a bit further. This troubled Ahluvya because she had forgotten everything since the Kundameanie spell. The MeeWee bird was trying to help and Ahluvya was trying not to fall back into anxiety over all of this, but the conflict in her heart was beating on her again.

"It's OK," assured Singya. She felt compassion for her loving sister who had no idea about Fergetcha and what had transpired on Mt. Iknowmenow. "Take your time, Ahluvya."

Ahluvya was comforted by Singya's kindness. For the first time since the spell she was willing to receive a gesture of goodwill from an outside source. It had been a long time since she had allowed her heart to take something in that was not hurtful.

She lay back down on the green grass and inhaled the sweet fragrance of the pink roses that surrounded their circle. Closing her eyes, Ahluvya took her first deep breath in a long time and tried to relax.

Since Useeme was still not functioning, it was hard for any of the sisters to visualize anything very clearly or to use their gifts of sensing without judging, so Ahluvya was left on her own to revive her heart's wisdom.

The beauty of nature's rhythms in the large open meadow eventually calmed Ahluvya into a trance-like state. She imagined that one of the pink rose buds lifted off of its bush and was floating toward her. She saw the rose stop in front of her and watched as it began to grow very large, opening its pink petals so wide that Ahluvya could step inside the center. The rose beckoned to her to do so.

Ahluvya could only slightly smell its sweet fragrance because Ivanna's senses were still numb, but the power of the rose felt so loving that the center of her own heart was beginning to shift as she imagined herself lying down inside the giant flower. The pink velvety walls enveloped her in this sacred space and she felt herself being cradled in the arms of a divine mother. She heard a soft voice that came from within her saying, "I trust my heart. I trust my heart. I trust my heart."

While drifting and relaxing even more inside the floating rose, Ahluvya finally felt the peace she didn't even know she had been seeking. Taking one long, full breath at a time, the heart chakra sister became very present with her surroundings. She knew she was inside her imaginary pink rose, lying on the grass in the ceremonial field. She knew that someone was nearby holding her in a pure intention of healing. She heard the sounds and smelled the smells of nature around her, and she could even detect the MeeWee bird softly continuing its call in sets of three, as if it were coaching Ahluvya to understand and remember something important.

Ahluvya knew these things without using her mind, but from the depth of feeling in her heart.

A distant, vague image of a green lotus blossom began to appear in her consciousness. Ahluvya moved into the picture that was forming and it brought back one of her first memories since arriving on Mt. Iknowmenow, when the seven chakra sisters were welcomed to Earth with their naming ceremony. Owl Woman had gifted her a green lotus flower to guide her through life and remind her of her natural birthright to love and be loved.

The steel door that Ahluvya had been hiding her heart behind began to melt a little. Her experience in the healing rose felt somehow familiar to her essence, but she still held on to small remnants of the fear that Fergetcha had instilled in her. Hatred was a cold and hard energy to release, even though Ahluvya was beginning to sense that something was transforming in her heart center.

She began to listen more intently now to the strange call of the MeeWee bird that seemed to be right outside her imaginary rose room.

"MeeWee. MeeWee. MeeWee!"

Mee. . . .Wee. . . Me. We. The song of ancient memory moved into Ahluvya. She began to piece together a few garbled words from the past . . .

"Your job, little center point, is to balance your sisters consciousness from 'me-thinking to we-being.' If not for you, the castle might collapse!"

In that moment, Ahluvya felt a shockwave of awareness shoot through her heart, like someone had plucked her decaying soul up from out of the bottom of a garbage dump into the bright light of day. She knew that something had been collapsing her heart, but now her memory told her that the whole castle was in grave danger.

"Move from me to we . . ."

"MeeWee. MeeWee. MeeWee!" The bird was persistent.

Ahluvya realized that she had not been giving her heart light to anyone. She had been living in isolation with her arms crossed across her chest, keeping her heart selfishly protected from the pains and fears of the world. She was not allowing any love to come in, either. Ahluvya was awakening from a nightmare and realized she was completely out of balance with her giving and receiving of love. Owl Woman had warned her about this and she had completely forgotten—until now.

"It has been all about me! Me. Me. Me. I've been so selfish. I haven't considered anyone else but myself. I forgot that we live in the castle together. If the whole castle is in trouble, it's all my fault!" she said as she started to revive herself from her meditation.

Ahluvya popped opened her eyes and stared at the girl with the wavy turquoise hair who was right by her side. "Singya!" was all she said. The chakra sister of sound was elated that her sister of the heart finally recognized her.

The MeeWee bird boldly hopped right up on Ahluvya's lap. "MeeWee. MeeWee. MeeWee!"

"Yes, I know, I remember now. I was living all alone, isolated and afraid. It was all about me, thinking only of me. I know I need to get well, but not just for me—it's also about all of our sisters. For the sake of the whole castle, we are a team!"

Ahluvya looked around at the women she assumed were her sisters, still lying on the ground around her, each in her own inner world of turmoil and concern. She met Owl Woman's dark, knowing eyes and started to remember this beloved guide, someone who loved and accepted her just as she was.

So strong was Owl Woman's love for the chakra sisters that she broke her own rule of nonattached witnessing to their healing and spoke. "Yes, Ahluvya, you are remembering now. The castle has been under hard times, but that is all an illusion! When you are steeped in the midst of it, you can't see it. But remember, this pain is not real. You and your sisters have only thought it was real. That's what the Kundameanie spell has been doing to you!" said Owl Woman, excited that she was finally breaking through Ahluvya's protective barriers.

"A Kundameanie spell?" questioned Ahluvya. "What are you talking about?"

"Ahluvya, that's what I've been trying to tell you all along!" said Singya, relishing the strength of her own voice again. "We have been put under a horrible spell and we all fell asleep. We forgot our true power. We lost our trust, our creativity, and our inner beauty. We forgot what peace feels like. We forgot how to love. We forgot each other! Ahluvya, you almost died!"

Singya was amazed at her ability to speak with such assurance. She could have recoiled in fear once again, believing that her words would be empty and meaningless, but she was speaking her truth, and this gave her the courage to continue. "Under this spell, all our sisters have gone their separate ways and have been miserable because of it. The spell from Fergetcha Kundameanie has made us forget the truth of who we are. We lost our intuitive senses and forgot how to follow the divine design of life."

"Singya, how do you know all of this?" asked Ahluvya.

"It was part of the spell from that distorted trickster. I tried to tell everyone, but no one would listen to me! Our sisters started telling lies, and we either began speaking harshly to one another or we didn't speak at all. We need help right now, Ahluvya, and you are the only one who can bring us back together. We need to *love* again!"

Ahluvya was still in shock about this whole idea. Owl Woman nodded her head to confirm what Singya had been saying. For the first time since the spells were cast, Singya felt validated and relieved and wanted to burst out with a raw, wild song but refrained in this moment of maturity, knowing that there were still five more sisters who also needed to be heard and validated for healing to take place. Singya was accepting the "we" part of what was transpiring.

"So now what do we do?" asked the sister of the heart, looking at her siblings who were strewn lifeless over the meadow. Singya and Ahluvya looked toward Owl Woman for some wisdom and guidance.

"We will work this out together tonight after the fire has been lit," said the wise creature woman, stalling so the sisters could find a way to shake off this gripping spell once and for all.

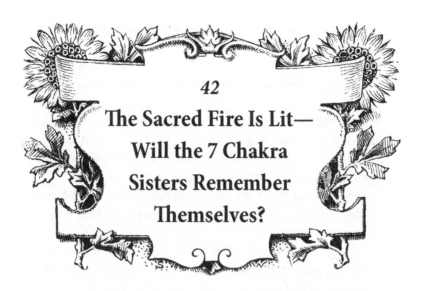

42
The Sacred Fire Is Lit— Will the 7 Chakra Sisters Remember Themselves?

The skies turned from turquoise to indigo as the sunset painted its pathway down into the horizon. Golden purple and red flames splattered through the distant pink clouds, signaling the beginning and the end of transformative energy on Mt. Iknowmenow. Whether it would be destructive or life-giving was yet to be determined.

The seven chakra sisters started to stir from their day-long healing reverie in the ceremonial field. One by one, they sat up feeling a bit more energized after their connection with Mother Earth. They looked toward the sacred fire that Owl Woman had prayerfully prepared. The stars were making their way through the dark sky, sprinkling the vast space overhead with infinite diamonds of light.

Each sister was drawn to the crackling warmth, and although they seemed to be walking in their sleep, they managed to find their way closer to the flames. Seven large tree stumps surrounded the sacred fire at the perfect height and distance for the sisters to seat themselves without feeling crowded while still being close enough to hear one another.

Being away from the castle and out in the elements for this brief time gave the sisters a new perspective, but Fergetcha's spell was potent and not so easily resolved. They still could not remember who the others were, and they all had mixed feelings and thoughts about the ancient elder who brought them here in the first place. Ahluvya and Singya were the only two who recognized Owl Woman's essence, but now they also remembered each other. It was the first step of moving from "me to we" that made their heart race and sparked a knowing within them of what they must do next.

Owl Woman paced around the outside of their circle, being mindful that she needed to take a minimal part in the healing process that would ensue.

Singya was still a little cautious since she was all too familiar with being ignored, ridiculed, and shut down by her sisters. She looked toward Owl Woman, who was focused on Ahluvya.

"I want to apologize to each of you," Ahluvya said to her beloved chakra siblings who encircled her around the fire.

"What for?"

"Do I know you?"

Singya shrugged and gave Ahluvya a knowing glance of how challenging it would be to get their sisters aligned again. So far, the sense of cooperation was nonexistent, though most of their normal tension was much less than it had been in the castle. A small stream of energy renewed by the elements of earth, water, sunlight, and air was beginning to move within the sisters.

"What are you sorry about?"

"Yea, what's this apology stuff?"

"I have let you down," confessed Ahluvya. "I have been so selfish. And in denying my own pain I have behaved very badly, thinking only of myself. The worst part is, I didn't ask for help when I needed it the most."

Ahluvya was pouring her heart out while her sisters were drifting away into their own self-centered and judgmental thoughts. She took a deep breath and continued, "I have been hiding from everyone. I'm sorry about not being available to love you through this horrible spell that we are under."

"Spell?" the others chimed in together.

"Oh no, not another bossy witch telling us more lies."

"Who is this chick, anyway?"

"What makes you so special?"

"I can't stand this anymore!" shouted Singya who had reached her limit with her sisters' negative and condescending attitudes. "Just once, I'm begging you to stop being so rude and arrogant! I know you are speaking from the spell's mindset, but quit asking stupid questions and get your acts together! Let Ahluvya speak. Please just shut up and listen to what she has to say without interrupting!"

The fire hissed and popped as Owl Woman tossed another log onto the flames, matching Singya's tone, who was also boiling inside and out.

Ahluvya felt the sting of this strange and difficult encounter with her sisters but found the courage to keep going this time rather than pull back. Even though her tone was harsh, Singya was helping Ahluvya find her own voice again.

"This spell is working because we have forgotten how to love! We have allowed something outside of us to cause fear and doubt. We have forgotten who we are! We are the seven chakra sisters. Yes, we *are* sisters," she added quickly.

"We are one body of energy. I need to love you—and myself, and you need to love yourselves and each other, too. But look—none of you even recognize each other. How can we love or live if we are separate from one another!? We need each other if we want to live! We have to work together!" pleaded Ahluvya. "This is urgent! We must wake up before our castle crashes forever!"

Ahluvya's newly revived passion carried her forward, "From what I can see so far, you are failing. You are all cowards, afraid to take a risk. Afraid to wake up and make a change in your lives. You are all in a stupor of fear and are being as selfish as I have been. Wake up!"

Ahluvya's heart filled with sadness as she said this. She wanted to be more loving, but she found herself becoming angry and judgmental toward her sisters. Was she fighting against them or for them? Was her heart truly loving her sisters, or was she selfishly speaking from a fear of her own death? It was all so confusing.

Ahluvya didn't know which sister needed to wake up the most to get things back in order. Singya could speak, but everyone else seemed either comatose or ready for combat.

Ahluvya turned to Useeme. "Wake up, Useeme! We need to get our thoughts right! No one can function without seeing a clear vision of our problem here." But Useeme still wasn't thinking clearly and denied that there was any problem at all.

"Iamone, help us find our way back to our source! We are lost without your connection to the universe. We need your energy, intelligence, and wisdom to guide us back together." Iamone was not in her wise witnessing mode; she was apathetic to Ahluvya's pleas for help.

"Oh Goddess help us! What's the matter with everyone? Wake up!" She ran to Aneeda and desperately started shaking her large, heavy body.

"Aneeda, you must pull Useeme and Iamone's energy down to earth so we can feel safe again! We can't be present without you. Focus!"

Aneeda's stomach rumbled, and she seemed clueless as to what Ahluvya was saying about feeling safe. Aneeda didn't feel like anything she could do would matter, and she was too afraid to try anyway.

Panic was rising up into Ahluvya's chest. "Ivanna, Ahafta, come on! Let's get moving!"

"What will you give me if I do?" asked Ivanna with a smirk on her face.

"I'm not moving anywhere just because you say so," harrumphed Ahafta, digging her heels into the ground.

Ahluvya was heartbroken. "I don't know what to do. Our castle is falling apart."

Singya was watching Ahluvya with empathy and saw herself doing the same things before. Purifying all her past pain into understanding, Singya finally intervened with as much truthful willpower as she could, coupled with the energy of love from her sister's heart of compassion. "Of course you know what to do, Ahluvya. You know our hearts. You are the closest to me, Useeme and Iamone, but you are also the closest to Aneeda, Ivanna, and Ahafta. You are the bridge that brings us together."

They both knew that Aneeda, Ivanna, and Ahafta were bound to the lower, slower vibrations of the physical world, needing and wanting power and material things. Singya, Useeme, and Iamone were mostly connected to the upper realms of higher thoughts and spiritual wisdom; they all needed each other to function at their full capacity. And Ahluvya was the sister in the center who bridged them all together. Ahluvya knew that she must live her purpose of loving unconditionally if the castle was to survive.

It didn't take long for Singya to find the right words. "Ahluvya, you have always led from your heart. Find your heart's greatest compassion now and our sisters will come around to you. There is no other vibration in the castle that can reach the lower and upper floors like your love."

"You are right, Singya. We need love, not scolding. Love is the only power that can break through our paralyzing fears. We must remember how to love ourselves first before we can move forward."

Ahluvya sat in quiet reflection for a while before she solemnly said, "This is the time for all of us to be devout catalysts for change."

Owl Woman smiled. The spell was weakening as Ahluvya remembered her power.

Ahluvya walked in a large circle around the blazing heat. Facing each sister one at a time she enticed them to remember the last time they were in this field, around this sacred fire.

A charge of radiant and radical love softened her tone as Ahluvya continued, "Sisters, I don't know what has happened to each of us, but I do know that we are all in big trouble. Apparently, the castle has been placed under a very bad spell of forgetfulness, and we need to adjust our calibrations and get back into alignment with each other. Each one of you must do what you can to change the energy—for yourself and for the whole castle. This is all about you, *and* it's not about you at all! Nothing can change until we all change. Each one of us is responsible for our part. The only way we can do this is by loving ourselves enough to care about something greater than our own individual problems."

Ahluvya took the seven long feathers that Owl Woman had saved from a previous ceremony and walked first to Iamone. Tapping Iamone on top of her head with the feathers, Ahluvya asked her to remember how it felt to be a reflection of divine consciousness. "Iamone, please remember. Open your mind. Let the light come in again."

With Singya's help, Ahluvya's voice poured out the purest love over Iamone's head. "It can be a very lonely and dull existence at the top of the castle when no one is around. I know how that feels. Iamone, you have six sister friends who are waiting to bring life back to you . . . but we need you to bring life back to them first! Open your skylights with your spiritually brilliant mind and let the universal energy come through again. It's your destiny, your purpose—*our* purpose. You are the divine connection to our source of all life!"

Ahluvya didn't want to be overbearing, but she knew this was her only chance to revive the other sisters. She kept tapping and then massaging Iamone on the crown of her head, hoping that would stimulate her memory of their beloved parents, the Queenking, their strongest connection to the great mystery of omniscient God-energy.

"Iamone, are you with me?"

Singya spoke up before anyone could protest. "Shhh, don't interrupt. What Ahluvya means to ask is if you understand that each one of us is connected to the others. She's not asking Iamone to follow her as if she is the leader. We can't work that way. We're all in this together. Before the sun rises, we must remember each other as a family. We need everyone to cooperate if we want to live!"

Owl Woman tossed another log onto the sacred fire, keeping the circle of sisters bathed in light. The darkness of night allowed each one to go within, seeing with inner eyes what they must understand to become whole again. The healings needed to be complete before the sun shone its full face, signaling their full remembering and awakening.

Ahluvya continued, "We have been made to feel separate from one another by a life-threatening Kundameanie spell that has placed our selfish egos above our connection to spirit. But none of us has the luxury of being self-indulgent anymore. We must help each other! We must wake up from this spell!"

The MeeWee bird chimed in with a loud "MeeWee!"

"That's right!" said Ahluvya, feeling lighter with the support of her exotic bird friend. "We must remember that we are a team, not individual me's!"

The sisters squirmed on their stumps, still stuck in their own selfishness and pain. Useeme spoke up first. "I'm listening, but nothing is really making any sense to me."

"Yes, Useeme," said Singya, "we know this sounds very strange, but this is the time we all must have a little trust. Sometimes we can't see what we need to believe, but please have faith in what we are telling you."

"Why should we trust you?" asked Ahafta, who had such low self-esteem that she couldn't get the big chip off of her shoulder.

Wise Iamone, whose crown had been stimulated by Ahluvya's love, answered this time. "Because having faith and trusting means we have to completely surrender to what is happening in this moment, while knowing everything is being orchestrated by a higher intelligence."

Ahluvya and Singya squeezed each other's hands excitedly, getting the first glimpse that Iamone might be waking up from her indifference to her sisters.

"Iamone, we love you, the Queenking loves you, all of your sisters love you, our beloved Owl Woman loves you, the entire universe loves you. Just look up at all those stars! Nothing but love could have created something so magnificent. Your true home has always been right here in this vast sea of love! Remember? The lower vibrations of the ego and limited mind do not exist in your world. Please open yourself to the universal light, Iamone. Let it shine through you again, to us, so that we can remember it too!"

Iamone's heart started to stir as she remembered Ahluvya's earlier words: "It's all about you, and it's not about you at all." She looked up at the infinite clusters of stars above her when her eyes landed on her favorite, Pleiades, the star system they called the Seven Sisters. She remembered her healing ceremonial flight into the moon shadow and back.

Reconnecting with the expansive mystery around her gave Iamone a new shot of energy. Her mind was filling with wonder rather than boredom, and she gazed out into space with a small but growing awareness of her part in the larger picture.

The fire silhouetted Ahluvya and Singya while they stood perfectly still, allowing Iamone plenty of time to awaken on her own. They had faith that her conscious thoughts would return to her higher purpose, and eventually back to remembering her natural state of bliss.

"Iamone, breathe! Breathe in long, slow deep breaths. Breathe in diamond clear-white light through the crown of your head. Breathe in your divine essence and focus on your union with the magnificence of this vast cosmos."

The duet of the heart and throat hoped that this would increase the flow of oxygen and energy within all the sisters and would help Iamone connect back to the spiritual nature of her essential self.

"Listen to the sounds of silence, Iamone. Silence . . . where you are the most comfortable. The universe is so still and quiet. Listen, it will help you remember who you are. This is your time to unite with the creative essence of all that is. Don't forget to keep breathing."

Singya and Ahluvya silently held the energy of stillness for a long, long time while Iamone recharged her cosmic batteries.

Singya finally whispered to Ahluvya, "We need to reach Aneeda, to make sure Iamone is grounded enough to not drift too far off into space. We can't lose her now."

Singya and Ahluvya were so concerned about their other sisters that they did not realize exactly when Iamone had slipped from her silent meditation into a deep transcendent state of being. In her mind, Iamone was reestablishing her union with the universe she once knew so well. She was moving from her mental concept of belief to a physical experience of faith to remembering that she was one with the consciousness of the universal Tribe of All-Knowing.

In her newly awakened state, Iamone was beginning to send energy through the airwaves that would assist all of the chakra sisters to remember their tribe again.

Ahluvya and Singya agreed to leave Iamone alone to absorb the unconditional love and healing energies from the universe.

"Who should we wake up next?"

"Well, we can't get through to Aneeda until Useeme sees that there is a problem in the castle," advised Singya.

"Aneeda isn't even aware of her unhealthy condition right now. We all need each other, but I'm spinning plates as fast as I can, Singya!"

"*We* are spinning these plates together, Ahluvya. Remember?"

Again they heard the little MeeWee chirping in agreement, which made them both deepen their appreciation for the tiny bird's profound message.

Ahluvya was running on pure love, which was the only energy that kept her going forward with any hope about the rest of her sisters. The fire snapped behind her. She knew that Useeme must be able to remember her own ability to visualize and think clearly so she could shed light on their situation. None of the chakra sisters could see the bigger picture of their need to change until Useeme saw it.

"Useeme, open your mind. Look at the fire. Keep looking until you can see all the colors dancing with the flames! Open your eyes, Useeme. Look closely."

Useeme was receiving a little bit of living energy now that Iamone was vibrating in her brain waves.

Singya started chanting a blend of mantra sounds, *hahm* and *om,* to empower her own resolve and that of her sister who lived one floor above her. Singya was the one to bring harmony to everyone, but like any chorus of mastery, she knew to layer one note upon the next. She broke her chant into four specific parts: *hah-oh-mm-*(silence). Singya's vibrations of her strengthening spiritual will-power were now blending with Ahluvya's seed sounds of the heart, *yahm-yahm-yahm.* These concordant tones of love from her sisters caused Useeme to feel a shift inside her mind. Her tension released as she became calmer.

"Useeme, look at the fire. What do you see?" asked Ahluvya. Singya kept chanting softly in the background.

"Bright white . . . like the light I've seen before somewhere. I see purples and royal blue. Wait, I remember the amethyst geode in my room! But I haven't seen it in a long time. Hey, where did that go?"

"Keep your focus on the fire, Useeme. What other colors do you see?"

Colors stimulated Useeme's vision centers. It was working. "Orange . . . no, it's gold! I see golden yellow light. And orange-reds, twisting with blue-purple. Wait . . . now I see a little green, like an emerald—only it's moving. It's really quite beautiful."

Useeme was still having a hard time staying focused, but Ahluvya and Singya kept chanting and encouraging her to stay present and keep her vision directed on one thing at a time.

"Yes, Useeme. Keep your thoughts disciplined. Clear your mind and keep focusing. You can see beautiful colors of our sacred fire dancing together, like all of your sisters! Remember?"

Useeme saw the shape of her loving heart sister standing in front of her now. The flames behind Ahluvya looked like an explosion of chartreuse and purple orchids stretching out and swaying in all directions. The two sisters held hands and the immediate contact of their energy reminded them of a vow they made long ago when they were given their names and purpose by their guardian, Owl Woman.

"Useeme, you *see* me!" shouted Ahluvya, hardly able to contain the love she was feeling deep in her soul. "I see you, too."

Singya intuitively shifted her chanting from the quiet stillness of om to the increasing sound of *ong . . . ong . . . ong,* which resonated with more activity for Useeme's third eye. This would keep her more awake and aware.

"Useeme, let the vibration of your indigo light connect you back to your Higher Self of intuitive wisdom. Iamone is right here to help." At this point, Singya and Ahluvya gave Iamone a strong nudge to bring her back into the circle.

Iamone watched as Singya brought her lips close to Useeme's forehead. "Let's sound together, *hmmmmm* . . . like a bumble bee. Keep your lips barely touching until you can feel them vibrate." The vibrations moved through Useeme's head and her tension released a little more. She began to roll her eyes in large circles while humming with her sister.

"Good, Useeme. Your eyes need to exercise so you can focus again."

"We know it's hard to move without Ivanna and Ahafta's energy, but try, Useeme. Let's do some gentle neck stretches. That will help our energy flow back into your mind."

As Useeme's neck and shoulders softened, Ahluvya reminded her to hold one nostril at a time, "Breathe, Useeme. Inhale from the right, exhale from the left. Now inhale from the left, exhale from the right. Do it again. Keep alternating, Useeme. You're doing great. Our brain needs oxygen!"

Ahluvya and Singya were feeling more energized as Useeme and Iamone started getting more clearheaded.

"This is our point of union, Useeme. Once you have awakened from the spell, you will bring your imagination and intellect back to the castle! We need your positive visionary abilities now more than ever, so we can see clearly and think wisely about where we are going. Help us make our decision to heal, Useeme. Time is running out!"

Tentatively, their delicate hands reached out to the other sisters. Iamone, Useeme, Singya, and Ahluvya were in a line now as the bond of the soul sisters on the upper floors made an unspoken but strong energetic reconnection.

Owl Woman was watching from a distance way up in one of the treetops, pleased with the unfolding of their own sacred ceremony so far.

It wasn't going to be quite as easy to reach the lower three sisters. They knew that Aneeda, Ivanna, and Ahafta were naturally more ego-centric, and more immersed in the material, physical realms of needs, wants, and personal power. Fergetcha's spell would have a stronger grip on their earthbound realities until they could break free from their attachments and fears.

Iamone, Useeme, Singya, and Ahluvya were collectively gaining an ability to perceive their dilemma of separation from Aneeda, Ivanna, and Ahafta. They watched the three younger sisters struggling to sit upright on the tree stumps, being distracted by the fireflies, the heat of the night, and the croaking crickets and frogs around them. They held aching backs and knees with their arthritic hands, trying to get comfortable.

Singya spoke first to Iamone and Useeme, who were finally beginning to respond with more clarity. Both Singya and Ahluvya were relieved to have their big sisters' spiritual maturity around them again.

"Aneeda has been wallowing in her self-defeating beliefs about not having enough of her needs being met. She has been too afraid to step out and receive the abundance of her gardens, or her sisters, or her friends in Thisismeville."

"Thisismeville!" gasped Useeme with the shock of remembering her larger sphere of family and friends. "Have they been under this spell, too?"

"What happens to the castle happens to everyone else," answered Iamone. "If our castle is falling apart, it must be affecting the whole community. We have let the townspeople down by our own forgetfulness. Without our collective connection with the universal intelligence, we have had no love, nor guiding wisdom."

"And our castle is crumbling because the foundation is getting weaker every moment that Aneeda stays in her stupor. If she continues to neglect her body, we will all suffer with weak immune systems and declining health. Aneeda must start taking care of herself! I'm sorry I didn't see this coming. Apparently I have been mindlessly wandering around the sixth floor," said Useeme, who was by now seeing the bigger picture of their impending demise.

"But Aneeda can't do anything until Ahafta gets her motivated. Aneeda has to get her lazy ass moving, and Ahafta's energy is what can save her," said Singya, getting bolder in her truthful way of saying what needed to be said about her ground floor sister.

"Well, that makes sense. Ahafta has to be next."

The four chakra sisters from the top floors now stood in front of Ahafta, their sister from the third floor. "Ahafta, you have to persevere! The castle is sick! Most of our dis-ease is from the mental and emotional stress that we have been under from Fergetcha Kundameanie's spell! You *have* to move, Ahafta, so we can get Ivanna and Aneeda moving again. We need your energy to get our energy back. You are responsible for that! You have to help us save the castle. We have to work together and you have to do your part, or we'll all die!"

Ahafta wasn't ready to surrender her control so easily. "Listen, all I know is that you can do everything in your life as perfectly as possible—do all the right things, and have a healthy lifestyle—but if someone stabs you to death, you're still dead! I'm not responsible for saving your castle, or these other two slackers," scoffed the stubborn sister, looking at a lifeless Ivanna and Aneeda. I didn't cause all these problems. It was an outside force. How do you expect me to fix it?"

Ahafta still wanted to blame someone else for what was happening, but her sisters weren't accepting any excuses. With Ahluvya's help, they considered their work to awaken Ahafta's independence as their act of devoted tough love for the whole castle.

"Look at this fire, Ahafta. You are the sister of the sun. Fire is your element. Get up! Move your willpower! Take a risk to make things better for yourself. Take a stand for your bold individuality, not your arrogance. Let this sacred fire burn away your inertia and doubts!"

With all their strength, they picked up Ahafta from her stump and carried her closer to the fire. "Soak it up, sister. Let the fire give you strength. Remember your courage, Ahafta. Come on, you can do this! Do it for yourself . . . for all of us. The whole castle needs you to realize that we all have to cooperate together. Remember who you are, Ahafta. Fire up your personal willpower! Remember your ability to always achieve what you want with certainty and excellence!"

They encouraged her to remember her breath of fire. "Pant like a dog! Be strong, Ahafta. We need your determination to get us out from under this horrible spell." They weren't giving her a chance to back down or protest.

The four sisters surrounded Ahafta, each in one of the four directions. Iamone stood to the north, Useeme to the east, Singya to the south, and Ahluvya to the west. "Breathe, Ahafta! You have to get the fire back in your belly, so the rest of us can feel good about ourselves again too!"

Singya repeatedly chanted the seed sounds for Ahafta's mantra, *rahm-rahm-rahm*. Ahafta wasn't given a chance to retort with her hot temper so she finally stuck out her tongue and found her rhythm breathing in and out, in and out. Owl Woman stayed in the background but began drumming to match Ahafta's steady panting pace with Singya's soul-centered sounds. *Rahm-rahm-rahm*.

The fire was leaping higher now, close to Ahafta's face. She closed her mouth and continued rapid and forceful breathing through her nose, focusing on the exhale, which contracted her belly. On her inhales, her belly expanded again.

"That's it. Keep going! Breathe the fire into your solar plexus, Ahafta. Inhale light. Exhale darkness! You taught us how to do this, remember? Good work, Ahafta!" Her older sisters were giving Ahafta everything she always used to do for them. They were working as a team, getting their gears in sync with increased energy and intensity, giving and receiving what each other needed for encouragement.

"Remember who you are, Ahafta—confident, courageous, unique! You are a master manifestor!" They cheered her on in harmony.

Ahafta's breath of fire got her energy moving and she was grateful to feel oxygen circulate through her again. As the third floor chakra sister slowed her breathing, she felt her vitality and strength return. With every breath, Ahafta was feeling her personal power radiate from the center of her solar plexus.

The impact of the Kundameanie spell was loosening its grip on Ahafta, but she still felt the traumatic blow in her gut. She walked back to the tree stump and sat down. Her sisters followed and sat down on the ground in front of her.

Ahafta looked at her four older evolved sisters who were now quietly giving her their total attention. "I'm embarrassed to tell you what I am thinking about myself," admitted Ahafta. "I'm so ashamed."

Her loving sisters didn't say a word, but Ahafta could feel their compassion flowing through her midsection, bringing more heat than the flaming fire burning behind them. Finally realizing what she had been doing on the third floor during a passage of timeless time under the spell, Ahafta spoke with a tone of regret, "I have been working myself to death . . . and killing the castle along with my need to feel important and powerful. I didn't feel good about myself; I thought I could never do anything right. I thought someone else would always do something better than I could. I kept hearing, 'Who do you think you are?' And it wasn't a memory of a warm, friendly voice either!" Her sisters nodded in agreement.

"I believed that voice. I didn't know who I was anymore. I compared myself to everyone else, which made me fiercely competitive, and if I thought I couldn't cut it I just gave up. I doubted myself. I believed I was a failure at everything, and I lost my self-confidence."

Ahafta was receiving Singya's energy and found the courage to keep speaking out loud. Her honesty was their golden treasure, and the sisters listened intently to Ahafta's self-reflections. "I forgot how to accept myself for just who I am. I thought I had to somehow prove that I was successful, that I was somebody."

Ahafta dropped her head down for a few moments, thinking before she continued. "All that wasted energy, trying to stay ahead of my poor self-esteem by pushing others around so I could be the big shot. What a weak-willed, arrogant way to behave! All this running on a treadmill has made me exhausted! What was I thinking?"

"You weren't thinking, Ahafta. That was all from the Kundameanie spell," said Ahluvya with her growing compassion.

"Please forgive me, Ahafta," apologized Useeme. "I too have been under Fergetcha's spell and I wasn't able to help you think clearly about anything you were thinking, or how you were behaving."

"I'm beginning to understand what happened to me," said the third floor chakra sister, who was finding her integrity again. "That spell was powerful. I know now that I can't find my identity through how much money I make, or what fancy title I have, or what I do for a living. I can't wait for someone else to approve of whatever I choose to do with my life. My true identity comes from a deeper place inside of me, not my ego." Iamone glowed when she heard this, knowing the truth of Ahafta's statement.

Useeme was seeing Ahafta's self-image getting stronger, and she focused on Ahafta's every word. "I have to be honest about who I really am, sisters. My friends in Thisismeville can think what they want, and although I respect them, their validation doesn't make me who I am. My status or title of Miss Responsible doesn't really make me feel important or special."

Ahafta continued, sitting a little taller now on her tree stump. "I can't believe in myself to make someone else think I've got it all together. I can only be competent for myself. I have to believe in myself for me! That's what makes me feel alive! That's who I think I am! In fact, I know who I am: confident and capable of doing anything—and I don't have to hurt or impress anyone else along the way!

Ahafta's spine straightened up even more. "I am happy when I can just be me. I am strong and determined to be who I am, right here, right now. I accept myself completely just as I am, sisters. And I'm not ashamed of that at all!"

Ahluvya's heart was wide open now, hearing how Ahafta was loving herself back to wholeness with her revelations. The sisters remained silent, smiling broadly while the fire roared behind them. They waited respectfully to hear if Ahafta had anything else to say.

Ahafta remembered that it was her responsibility to help her chakra sisters take all necessary and appropriate actions to move forward in life. She finally spoke with her sincerest authority, "Who am I? What is my main purpose? I am me no matter what. I *have* to put myself out into the world, to be reliable with full integrity and honesty. It is my destiny to empower myself first and foremost, then my sisters, the castle, and everyone I encounter."

Ahafta's voice got louder with each declaration, "I have the right to move in the world as myself! I have to live on purpose . . . to be *me*."

Ahafta looked at Ahluvya, knowing that her personal power was only effective when it came with loving intentions. She paused for a moment as the MeeWee bird started to squawk again. She understood its message. "Yes, I get it. I am only me when all of my sisters are fully themselves, too. It is really we that makes me, me."

With that revelation, Ahafta let her inner fire roar. "So listen up, Fergetcha Kundameanies of the world," she shouted to the stars above. "I remember who I am! I will fight for my castle's survival! I will not die with any regrets! I am essential urgency energy!"

Owl Woman chuckled from her perch high in the canopy of trees that surrounded this scene. She knew that Ahafta's healthy self-controlled ego definitely had its place. If the sisters were to bring their enlightened thoughts into the world, Ahafta was the go-getter, the action-oriented sister with the passion and urgency to get what mattered done.

The energy was getting stronger around the circle when Ahafta intuitively picked up on their thoughts about the fire in her belly. "Hey, my stomach feels much better. Thanks, sisters!"

That made them all jump up and slap each other on the backs, giving high fives and hollers of achievement.

"Come to think of it, the pain in my chest has lifted and my heart feels much lighter," said Ahluvya.

"My throat isn't sore anymore," said Singya.

"My focus is more clear, and my eyes aren't blurry!" said Useeme.

"My headache is finally gone!" said Iamone, relieved.

Satisfied with their accomplishments so far, but still not quite grounded yet, the five sisters now turned to Ivanna and Aneeda, who had not participated in any of this hoopla around the fire.

Ivanna had experienced the biggest emotional crisis of them all. Her vacillating moods affected everyone, but at least her sisters on the upper floors were maintaining a better focus on their situation now. They were trying to ignite their own energy frequencies to help Ivanna deal with her unhealthy attachment to drama.

Each chakra sister felt the pain of Ivanna's need to numb herself to escape her emotional turmoil. Ivanna's guilt over experiencing any kind of pleasure was having a negative effect on all of them, and her addictions were keeping their energy stuck in a destructive cycle.

"I didn't realize how much I've been missing Ivanna's joy."

"You're right, Ahluvya. I've been so stuck in my need to be overly responsible that I lost my enthusiasm for doing anything. I just couldn't feel Ivanna's liveliness on my floor, either. Having healthy relationships with others is more important than I realized. I've missed having fun with my friends," admitted Ahafta.

"I hear you, Ahafta," said Singya. "Every time I tried to express myself, I felt a huge burden bearing down on me. We really need Ivanna to bring back her creative juices again. Without her, we are just depressed, bored, and unexcited about life."

"I see what you are saying, sisters. Our thoughts have been in conflict with our feelings. That's what happens when we are out of alignment with each other," said Useeme.

"My nightmares must be tied to Ivanna's guilt, too. If she is not having any pleasurable experiences, then I am sure to continue dreaming and imagining all sorts of negative things. We must help Ivanna see how her unpredictable energy and addictions are bringing the whole castle down."

Iamone was opening her portals to the higher dimensions during this conversation. "The only way to overcome addiction is to turn to the Spirit of Life and surrender all unconscious attachment to pain. Ivanna must first recognize that she is under a spell.

"She has been believing lies about herself, as we all have been doing. If each one of us opens our channels to universal wisdom, we will remember the truth of who we are in the highest spiritual sense. We can send that energy down deep into Ivanna's abdomen, where she is suppressing her true feelings and holding all of her guilt."

Ivanna paid no attention to what her sisters were saying. She was doing a two-step tango in her own head to occupy her time while sitting on her wood stump. "It takes two, baby, me and you . . .

ooo-ooo. . . . Dark and light, day and night. Good and bad, happy and sad . . ." It didn't take much for Ivanna's emotional moods to shift, so simply hearing herself say the word "sad" made her start to cry. She was oblivious of her sisters' healing processes during the night and was absorbed in her own up-and-down emotions.

Useeme agreed with Iamone's wise spiritual assessment, but she could see Ivanna's dilemma from another perspective and tried to explain it a different way to her sisters. "Living on the second floor of the castle gives Ivanna double trouble. She thinks in twos, always living in the tension and duality of opposites. Black and white. Male and female. Positive and negative. The sun and the moon. Two is the number of balance, but also of conflict and opposition. The spell of forgetfulness has amplified these polarities for Ivanna, and she is not comfortable with either direction that she faces."

"Useeme," said Ahluvya, "Ivanna needs to be OK with the natural yin and yang of the world. You are the one who can help her get this paradox balanced and integrated again, right?"

"Oh, there's a pair of docs here!? Where are they?" asked Ivanna, perking up as she overheard the conversation around her.

Useeme just shook her head at Ivanna's spacey response and answered Ahluvya, "Once I fix the computers on my floor, I can reprogram the miraculous neuroplasticity of the whole system and it will rewire itself. Then new synapses will repair all our broken connections with higher conscious thoughts again."

Hearing this gave all the sisters some hope that the castle actually could come back to its natural sense of enlightened living.

"I wasn't sure why I always felt seasick," said Ahafta, "but I know now that it has been from Ivanna's wild ride on her turbulent ocean of emotions. Singya, you'll be able to bring harmony back to Ivanna's discordant feelings, right?"

Ahluvya also understood relationships, like Ivanna did, but she knew that if Ivanna was going to maintain healthy friendships then she had to set clear boundaries and stop allowing others to step all over her. "I'll help Ivanna learn to stop manipulating others, too."

The five sisters circled around Ivanna and generously poured their sympathetic and loving energy over her, like Iamone suggested.

Iamone and Useeme talked as one sister, united in their purpose of awakening their little sister who lived on the second floor. They spoke to Ivanna in a serious tone, but made sure that compassion was heard in their collective voice with the help of Singya and Ahluvya.

"Ivanna, do you understand that we have been put under a very destructive spell? No one is to blame, but our castle is in grave danger of collapsing." Knowing how sensitive Ivanna could be, they chose their words carefully to keep any extreme emotions from erupting.

"We're not exactly sure what happened to you, but no one in the castle has been acting normally since Fergetcha Kundameanie caught us off guard. We have been separated from one another, and each of us has suffered in our own way."

Ivanna bolted upright. "Fergetcha? Why does that sound familiar?"

"What matters the most right now is that you begin to take back your power, Ivanna. You have given yourself over to the whims of your volatile emotions and it is affecting all of us in a negative way."

"Volatile emotions!? Who said that to me? Where have I heard that accusation before?" gasped Ivanna, recalling a split-second moment before she was taken prisoner by a strange woman with sparkly scarves.

"Oh no . . . I knew it! This is all my fault. I'm such a bad girl. I left the castle without you. I'm so ashamed of myself. I am guilty for all our problems! I've lost your respect. I feel . . . I feel . . . Oh, I don't know what I feel! I need a drink or a pill to calm my nerves. Anyone have an antidepressant? I just want to kill myself."

"Stop it, Ivanna!" shouted all of her sisters, as if they had just given her a galactic smack in the face. "Stop feeling so sorry for yourself. Discipline your thoughts! You cannot solve your uncomfortable feelings with alcohol or drugs or sugar or shopping!"

"Ivanna, I've got to tell it to you straight," said Singya as honestly as she could. "You've forgotten how to feel safe expressing your feelings, and you've acted out in ways that are not healthy for you. Face it, your addictions and attachments are killing you, and all of us, too. You must get a grip on your life right now or we will all go down the mountainside in one emotional heap of destruction!"

Ivanna wanted to lash out at Singya and withdraw at the same time. She couldn't find any middle ground to stand on. She began weeping uncontrollably again.

The five princess sisters had thought they were getting through to Ivanna, but they were stuck about how to help their emotionally unstable sister now. Iamone and Useeme reminded everyone to hold Ivanna in the image of her Higher Self, connected to the oneness of all. Singya reiterated that they needed to speak their truth with understanding and kindness. Ahluvya reminded them to refrain from scolding and to open their hearts with love and compassion for their struggling sister, even if she was oversensitive and exaggerating her melodramatic moods. Ahafta was revving up her internal motor to get Ivanna to physically move beyond her emotional outbursts.

In the background, Owl Woman started to shake her healing rattles and bells to change the uncomfortable energy in the charged air. The moving rhythms began to stimulate Ivanna's sensual hips. The five sisters picked up on that and lifted Ivanna off her seat to do a slow belly dance with her, swaying gracefully like swans swimming in a beauty pageant.

Singya repeatedly chanted the seed sounds, "*vahm, vahm, vahm*," for Ivanna to reactivate her vivacious energy.

As they danced, they led her away from the fire and down to the stream, walking their little emotional sister right into the flowing waters. Ivanna shivered with the shock of the cold bath, but it refreshed her memory of pleasant times when she used to flow easily with the current under these starlit skies.

The sisters washed Ivanna's auburn hair and scrubbed her clean while they whispered soft affirming messages of serenity. "There, there, Ivanna. It's OK. Just feel our love, sister, and feel your own precious love. It's wonderful to enjoy the pleasures of the senses. Love your body, love your emotions. Feel the calm waters flowing over you, Ivanna. Relax and let your joy return. Allow the beauty of life to flow through you."

The water poured in undulating ripples over Ivanna's head, dripping onto her dehydrated body. She soaked up the adoration and attention she was getting. The familiar soothing waters helped her release the tension and anxiety she had been feeling for so long. She was beginning to feel her sisters' love again, the first step toward breaking the spell.

After washing their own hair in the cleansing waters, Iamone, Useeme, Singya, Ahluvya, and Ahafta wrapped Ivanna in a fluffy robe and escorted her back to the fire where she warmed her aching body. They massaged her with her favorite oils of jasmine and rose until her stiff lower back and rigid knees finally softened.

"Remember how easy it is for you to have close relationships with so many good friends, Ivanna. Especially with us. We love you, sweet sister."

Ivanna felt much more in control of herself and everyone sighed in relief.

"OK, now that Ivanna is calm we can have a real conversation about our situation, because nothing gets resolved when our emotions are flying all over the place," said wise Iamone.

"Ivanna, your job is to keep feeling all of your feelings, but in a balanced way," said Ahluvya. "Let your emotions flow through you, don't let them get stuck inside! But don't flood your floor with tears either, because that's not safe for any of us in the castle."

"There is no need to ever feel guilty about your birthright to enjoy pleasure, Ivanna. Guilt is a trick of the Kundameanie spell. It's not part of your true energy. Remember how great you feel when your natural senses of joy and enthusiasm are unleashed?"

"Our sisters are right! It is perfectly fine for you to feel whatever you feel, Ivanna, whether it is sadness or grief, or even toxic emotions like fear, jealousy, or anger."

"And it's even better to feel something that wakes up your cells, like happiness! Emotions make you, you, Ivanna!"

"And the best part of being able to feel everything," said Useeme with her wide-angled view, "is that you get to choose how long you want to feel it. You get to decide, with my help, whether you move toward something destructive or something healthy and life-giving; whether you dwell in muck and stay stuck or be well by letting your feelings flow forth."

"I can dwell—or be well," Ivanna repeated in her head.

"Ivanna, isn't it true that choosing to feel good is effortless and natural for you, without having to take any artificial happy pills?"

"Stay away from those false mood enhancers, Ivanna, and before you know it you'll be loving all the yummilicious pleasures of life again!"

Ivanna looked at her amazing sisters and remembered her relationships with all of them. They hugged each other, squeezing tightly. Ivanna vowed to keep healthy boundaries around herself for the sake of the whole castle. She promised to continue to look within for stronger self-discipline, and to be more adaptable to the changing waters in the river of life. Best of all, Ivanna knew she had her team of chakra sister cheerleaders for support if she ever felt out of sorts again.

Iamone had some final words of wisdom for Ivanna. "My job is to make sure all of us live in the spiritual consciousness of oneness and connectivity to all. However, I do understand that the world of duality and separateness is real, at least on the earth plane of humanity. All of our sisters, especially me, need to feel our soul's satisfaction, to experience the world through the living senses . . . and you navigate that better than any of us, Ivanna!"

This statement from her big sister made Ivanna feel validated and special.

"Duality is what it is, but we don't have to let that fact separate us, as long as we are aware of it," added Useeme, remembering the two separate but equally important wings on her sixth floor of the castle. "I will help you balance and integrate all the opposite forces in your life, Ivanna, so the castle can remain in homeostasis. Just remember that we can't see the light of the stars unless there is darkness for the contrast. It's all good, even the part you call 'bad.' Comparisons are how you measure things, like this or that, up or down, here or there."

"Or which color sweater compliments my new skirt the best?!" said Ivanna, showing that she understood Useeme's teaching in her own way.

"Fortunately," said Ahafta, "I have learned that comparing myself to others is a useless waste of energy. I will make sure that comparing one thing to another will move you forward and toward the healthiest choices for your life, Ivanna!"

"I will help you say yes or no to those choices, and to mean what you say!" said Singya. "I'll be right with you when you want to set those healthy boundaries for yourself, Ivanna."

"Duality is also useful in relationships," added Ahluvya, patiently giving Ivanna plenty of time to absorb her lessons, "so you can know which friends feel the most comfortable to be around, and who to stay away from, since everyone is different."

"And as for sex . . . " Ahluvya continued, "I will help you remember to not close your heart for selfish reasons or instant gratification—or out of fear of loving altogether. When your heart is communicating with my heart, then sex becomes a holy and sacred act that deepens a meaningful relationship. Ivanna, you are wired to enjoy the love that is possible when you maintain healthy boundaries for yourself! Healthy sexuality is a marriage of two hearts that can truly love in union. When you make healthy choices for yourself in right relationships, guilt cannot enter your energy field."

Useeme's increasing clarity of mind helped Ivanna understand her situation and to see it for herself. "Remember, Ivanna, guilt is only a Kundameanie illusion. Come up to the sixth floor to see me and when you are in my room, I'll help you control your 'vroom-vroom' energy by keeping you mindful of your many desires!"

Ahluvya's heart expanded when she added, "Before you know it, your creative urge to merge will mature into a co-creative regeneration of the castle's life force for all of us to enjoy!"

The girls broke into laughter at all the sex talk. As they settled, Iamone spoke again. Her lavender white aura expanded, and everyone could touch the sensations of universal energy from their most spiritually advanced sister. "This is important, Ivanna. I want you to visit me every day on the seventh floor. In addition to our daily purification and meditation, I will help you surrender the ego to our creator, where your earthly concerns do not exist. We'll connect with the universe's unlimited divine love, which will always bring you back to your truth. There is no such concept as guilt when you remember to connect with your truest spiritual essence. You are not being judged ever, Ivanna. Love yourself just as you are, little sister. Castle life is no fun without you!"

Ivanna pulled her sisters close to her again and they hugged in one large mass.

Owl Woman made sure that the sacred fire was stoked high enough to help them burn away the Kundameanie spell completely. Feeling strong and much more empowered by the firelight, the six chakra sisters turned now to Aneeda, who had unknowingly slumped off her stump. She was snoring, snorting, and drooling on the ground.

43
Mom and Dad Start Breathing Heavy— and There's Nothing Sexy About It

Meanwhile, back at the castle, the last board was falling through the broken foundation floor, the banister was hanging by a nail, and shards of crystals dropped away from the cracked windows. There was no energy in the castle, no water flowing, no fire burning, no air to breathe, no sounds, no light, no thought. It was more of a casket than a castle.

Fergetcha Kundameanie had moved back into town during the dark of night. Assuming that the seven chakra princesses had simply withered away, she set herself up in the broken castle. She was so absorbed in her own victimhood and complaints about how dreadful life was that she didn't lift a finger to clean up the mess that surrounded her.

Fergetcha was confident that her spells would destroy the castle once and for all. She didn't care if it collapsed right under her, but at least for now it was cheap rent. The presence of her malignant energy made the crystal structure dislodge from Mt. Iknowmenow at an increasing rate. The foundation was tearing away from the walls of the supporting rock, and cracking sounds of the break-up could be heard over the land. The mountain itself was grieving the loss.

The Queenking could feel the effects of the turbulent Kundameanie energy that had entered the castle during the night. Filled with compassion and concern at the same time, they said, "We've waited as long as possible. We cannot stand by and just observe this disaster. We will need to intervene to keep the castle standing. Our daughters depend on the health of the entire system. All of Thisismeville is depending on it. We have called for assistance, but we will have to take matters into our hands now."

The Queenking had to slow his-her vibrations, deliberately moving from unity to duality, in order to enter the castle. With the golden staircases falling down and Iamone's skylights sealed shut, they had to use the emergency shoot. The clear column of light in the center of the spiral staircase was the only thing in the castle that was not harmed by the Kundameanie spell. It was the most direct line of energy between the universe and the Earth, but its life-giving force was only activated when the seven chakra sisters touched it with their consciousness on their journey up the spiral staircase. The Queenking broke the rules in this case. In less than a figment of imaginative time, Mother Queen and Father King were on the ground floor of the disintegrating castle.

"Empty. It's completely void of life's energy here! Where are our princess daughters? I feel like I'm suffocating."

"Heh heh heh," clucked Fergetcha from the crumbling foyer of the first floor. As the regal parents turned around they saw their nemesis with arms folded, leaning up against the rusty red clunker convertible.

"Looks like the young ones have left the nest, folks. What a shame. But I'm here now, so don't you worry your little royal heads. Everything will be in my hands from now on," Fergetcha said as she waved her hand in a dismissive gesture.

Another bolt dislodged from the spiral staircase as Mother Queen's energy began to steam throughout her consciousness. The illusion of separation was already moving between the royal parents and the wicked spellcaster.

"Well, if it isn't Fergetcha of Kundameanie fame, right here boldly in our midst. We know what you have been up to, and of course you know that we must and will protect that which we love. This castle is life-giving, and we are quite aware of the illusion of death that you have created for our daughters."

Father King was in no mood to struggle with the pathetic woman either. "We command you to leave these premises right away, Fergetcha. . . . And take your dismal energy with you!"

Fergetcha guffawed so loudly that the remaining crystal walls imploded from the top floor, crumbling down seven flights in a thunderous roar.

44

It All Rests on Aneeda Now—Remembering Who's Who

Back at the ceremonial fire, the six chakra sisters hovered over Aneeda, feeling pity and compassion for their sister with the raven black eyes who now seemed so out of her element and her body.

The first hint of sunrise blended a pink tint into the slightly graying sky. They knew their collective healing so far would not last if there was no secure foundation to build upon. Aneeda held the last and most important key.

Aneeda started to rouse just a little when she heard all the sisters speak amongst themselves about their awareness. "We agree now that our lack of energy has been caused by a Kundameanie spell. We know that we forgot our true power and allowed fear to rule over our destiny of love and unity. But right now, we have to take responsibility for the growing cancer that is consuming our castle!"

"We have been eating ourselves up with all of our fears, doubts, lack of self-love, lack of hope, lack of self-respect, and our disrespect to each other."

"Instead of living with loving abundance, our castle has been filled with toxins and poisons—from what we have been consuming, from unnecessary chemicals we've been ingesting, from looking for quick fixes for our problems, but mostly from what harmful thoughts we've been thinking, and negative emotions we've been feeling."

"With Aneeda down like this, we don't have a leg to stand on."

"We can't put one foot in front of the other."

"Poor Aneeda. . . . She just doesn't feel safe anywhere. She has been seriously wounded."

"But she's gotten comfortable in her laziness, and we can't afford to fall back now. She needs to move out of this dangerous comfort zone, and quick!"

Aneeda stirred and pushed her large, round body up, leaning against the tree stump for support. Her sisters did not want to sound judgmental or condescending, but their gears still weren't in sync from heaven to earth yet.

"Aneeda, our castle is collapsing! There is no foundation left to hold anything up, much less build upon."

"We need your energy to root us to the ground again!"

"We also need your initiating energy to get things moving upward in the castle!"

"Now I know why I felt like I had to throw my weight around on the third floor," said Ahafta. "Look at yourself, Aneeda! You have limited your fearful existence to the kitchen—and not because you've been cooking anything healthy, apparently!"

"You've been filling your insecurity and feelings of emptiness with junk food and meaningless clutter. Our castle cannot function until you get back on your feet!"

"You are giving your power—*our* power—away, Aneeda! Stop it!"

"Come back to the rest of your sisters, Aneeda, or we're all going to die!"

Aneeda couldn't distinguish this onslaught of hurtful words from her encounter with Fergetcha. She only heard tones of condemnation, which caused her to pull back with more angst and fear.

Owl Woman was intuitively sensing distress from both the scene at the sacred fire and the ruckus that was happening back at the castle. Time was running out, but their magical guardian still had hope that the seven chakra sisters could work this out on their own. Once a sacred ceremony like this had begun, Owl Woman knew the spell could be broken only if healing took place before the first breaking light of dawn.

"Love, girls. We must remember to heal our wounds with love. It's the only medicine that will work against these deadly spells," reminded Ahluvya. They all agreed for the first time, and that made the MeeWee bird very happy.

Ivanna was the closest to Aneeda, and her own healing was just sinking in to her consciousness. Kneeling down low to the ground beside her first floor sister, Ivanna held Aneeda's feet firmly and stared into her eyes to give her complete attention. Even though Ivanna's awakening was so fresh, her memory was almost fully reengaged and she recalled that Aneeda was not only her sister, but also her best friend and companion. Ivanna recalled how apprehensive they both were when they kept being bombarded by all of their unsuspecting siblings falling on top of them when they were back at the castle.

Before Ivanna said anything, she felt Ahafta giving her courage and Ahluvya opening her heart. Singya's vibrations added a backdrop of sounds as she helped with Aneeda's mantra, repeating "*Lahm, lahm, lahm.*"

Useeme was giving Ivanna the ability to focus her mind and think clearly. She was integrating her understanding with Singya's creative expression so she could be discerning in her choice of words. Iamone was simply radiating her all-knowing energy through all of her sisters, which created the strong unifying force field that was needed to assist Aneeda's breakthrough.

"Aneeda, you are safe with me. I'm Ivanna, your sister who lives one floor above you in the castle. I love you, Aneeda. I've missed you. You don't have to protect yourself anymore with your excess body shield. You are safe with all of your sisters now. Please come back so we can play again. I need you . . . *we* need you!"

Aneeda was disoriented, but she seemed to be listening. Her team of sisters took a different approach this time, although they were feeling the impending impulse to hasten their work since daylight was rapidly approaching.

"Aneeda, remember these?" cajoled Ahafta, giving her a bouquet of the red wildflowers brightening the field around them. "It's your favorite color, red!"

Ahluvya gave Aneeda a handful of terra-cotta stones, encouraging her to remember what she loved most, "Look, Aneeda, your favorite red rocks!"

Singya kept on chanting *lahm, lahm, lahm* in the background, keeping the rhythm slow and steady. The sisters knew that Aneeda would resonate with anything that was solid and simple, so they monitored their pace with the dense pull of gravity even though they could see the morning mist of dew through the rising sunlight. The six princess sisters were gravely concerned for their dangerously disintegrating home.

Useeme tugged at some wild red radishes that were tucked in with the flowers and handed them to her sister, "Roots! Aneeda, remember your roots!"

Iamone was the link to their Heavenly Mother, but they needed Aneeda to anchor that cosmic energy at the opposite end. Iamone reminded Aneeda, "Mother Earth is here, holding you now. Feel her heaviness and her support. You are safe in her arms." Hearing the word "mother" made Aneeda cry, but at least she was beginning to feel a little more secure and stable.

"Feel your body. Move your energy down your legs, deep into the earth, Aneeda. Remember how good that feels! You need to grow strong roots again. We need you to anchor us together, Aneeda!"

"That's it . . . way down into the ground. You are best at being our little rooter. Dig deep. Trust us." Aneeda moved a few inches away from her tree stump and realized she was surrounded by her sisters who were all kneeling next to her now.

"Mother Earth gives you everything you need, Aneeda. You just need to remember. Close your eyes and remember. See the abundant nourishment that Mother Earth gives you. It is endless. There is plenty, and you always have enough."

Useeme could envision her root chakra sister's excess weight falling off of her when she said, "Feel your body melting down and merging with the earth, Aneeda. You can let go of any excess weight that might be keeping you in prison. Don't be afraid. Be strong, Aneeda. Your sisters are right here with you. You are safe. You don't need to protect yourself anymore. We will always stay connected to you. But now we need you to ground us back to Mother Earth."

Energy was swirling around the fire as the last of its luminosity flickered in a soft blue and maroon frame.

"You have every right to be here, Aneeda. We love you and accept you just the way you are. You can trust life again. You are safe and secure. We are right here with you. Feel the earth beneath you, Aneeda."

Aneeda shifted her weight and began to enjoy the sensations moving through her body again. She pulled her knees to her chest and then stretched her legs out long, feeling her feet twist around at the ankles. She was beginning to remember herself.

The healing process could not be rushed, and the sisters were aware of Aneeda's need to awaken in her own time. At the same time, knowing she needed to move a little more quickly, the sisters offered another suggestion. "We'll help you remember your favorite standing yoga pose!"

Ivanna and Ahafta held Aneeda's feet to the ground and Ahluvya embraced her in the middle, pulling her torso up off the ground. Singya lifted her right arm and Useeme lifted her left arm until her both of her hands were high over her head. Iamone lifted

Aneeda's head up just enough to allow her neck to elongate, aligning her spine so all of their energy could flow through her from head to toe.

"Let the base of your spine relax. Open your hips, Aneeda. Breathe all the way down to your tailbone. Let your large bones settle down into their proper place. Feel how strong you are! Now focus on your legs . . . and your feet. . . . That's it! Come back to your true body. Please, Aneeda. The whole castle needs you."

Colors, images, feelings, thoughts, and a powerful wave of love started to take shape within Aneeda's consciousness. She heard soothing frequencies in her mind which drowned out the fearful remnants of Fergetcha Kundameanie's voice. Iamone's portals to the Great Spirit were open, and it was speaking directly to Aneeda. "Aneeda, I have given you all that you need. You, and you alone, are responsible for your healing. But there is help all around you. It is your choice to remain asleep in a dead weight stupor, or wake up to the fullness of life once again." The ground floor chakra sister quivered when she heard this, but she knew it was coming from an abundantly loving universe.

Standing very still now, Aneeda relaxed her arms and shoulders. Her legs felt strong as the communication between the voice of wisdom and Aneeda continued. "Take care of yourself, Aneeda. Do not wait for someone else to clean up your mess. Take responsibility; see the truth of what is happening to you. Stay grounded, steady as a rock. Be solid. You are secure, but remember that you can always run as fast as lightning when you need to!"

The red rock rooted sister began breathing her strength back into her foundation.

Daylight was climbing over the expansive landscape and the sky was getting a little brighter. The sacred fire was almost out, and Owl Woman knew that their crystal castle was on a very precarious edge. The seven chakra sisters needed to return to Mt. Iknowmenow as one team working in unison if the castle was to survive. It was closer to the dawn of a new way of living than anyone realized.

They could feel the lands around Mt. Iknowmenow and Thisismeville shaking underneath them from the disturbance of energy back at the castle. It toppled Owl Woman from the branches and she crash-landed to the ground, which caught everyone's attention.

A brisk early morning breeze blew Ahafta's golden mane across her face. The sister of fire sensed the urgency of the moment and her energy translated that feeling to all the sisters. Everyone looked at Aneeda, whose belly now laid flat on the ground. She put her ear to the earth, listening to the implications of the threatening vibrations that were emanating from beyond.

The winds picked up as the sun was edging upward over the horizon. Owl Woman's feathers were standing on alert, flapping with persistent pressure over their serious situation. Aneeda reached out for Singya and Useeme's hands to help her listen and decipher the meaning clearly. She heard a familiar voice in the trees and the thick grasses beneath her, a sound which originated from the core heartbeat of both heaven and earth. All seven chakra sisters had their energy portals open, each willing to receive any helpful messages from above and below which would be for Aneeda's best benefit and greatest healing.

Aneeda remembered her purpose and was getting a clear message for herself. She kept listening in silence until awakening thoughts sped through her mind. "I remember now. . . . Red. Rocks. Roots. My sisters will not live very long if I don't batten down the hatches. It's up to me. I am the rock they stand upon. I need to feel my body fully alive and healthy again! I need my own inner peace and stability so my sisters can depend on me to be strong for them. I am their foundation. I need to take responsibility for myself, be the gatekeeper, to start the life force rising up to the upper floors of the castle! I need to send vital energy through the entire castle system, otherwise we are all doomed." Aneeda remembered Oimalive Fundalini's lessons about igniting the castle's first light.

The others were exercising great patience while they waited for Aneeda to respond. Owl Woman paced around the fire, which was crackling quietly as the red charcoals lay naked in grey ashes, no longer on fire but not yet cool.

"I remember now how much we need each other!" said Aneeda, bolting upright. Speaking out loud for all of her sisters to hear, Aneeda gathered her red rock root strength and interpreted her silent inner message. "I need to be physically strong and healthy from the earth, but I need all of my sisters for our nourishment to be complete. Our bodies need the energy of the plants on earth. That's my job, to eat well and exercise—but the plants need water to flow in order to grow, which is Ivanna's job."

"And life on earth has to have the sun's energy, which is my job," added Ahafta.

"And my purpose is to breathe oxygen into that life," said Ahluvya, "so the earth, water, fire, and air can feel the love of our synergy working together."

Singya chimed in, "I help us pull it all together with the songs and sounds of nature—of the birds, the oceans, the fires, the winds, and the messages from our intuitive inner voice."

"And sisters, once your energy reaches us on the top two floors, we connect our family energy of the castle to the source of all . . . to this life on earth, our galaxy, and the many universes beyond."

"So we can merge with the ultimate divine light and remember our higher consciousness and connection to all that is," said Useeme and Iamone, finishing each other's sentences.

"We are one!"

"When we work together, we can be the peaceful presence that we were meant to experience. So no more fighting amongst ourselves, sisters, right? When we live in harmony together as One Being, our unified peace gives us our good health, emotional stability, inner security, joyfulness, intelligence, and enough love to heal the castle, the town of Thisismeville, and the whole world!"

Owl Woman heaved a huge sigh of relief and the MeeWee bird skipped around the circle, singing its song and awakening the day as all the other birds chimed into the morning chorus. The seven chakra sisters remembered who they were as they created their own field of coherence and cooperation. Holding hands, their collective heat burned away the morning fog. The white golden sun had fully emerged over the eastern horizon, throwing long shadows over the circle of the seven chakra sisters.

Fergetcha's spell had lost its tight grip on them, but there was no time for celebrating. Suddenly remembering the dire state of their decomposing castle, all the sisters agreed at once with one word which completed Aneeda's healing: "*Run!*"

They knew, like their parents, that they would and must protect what they loved and valued more than anything. They ran back to their crystal castle with the strength and passion of seventh heaven in their legs, with Aneeda leading the way. So determined was their desire to save their precious castle that they ran with the same blast of integrated energy that birthed the seven colors of the rainbow, actually outrunning Owl Woman's flight across the land. They even made time to speed purposefully in seven intersecting circles, creating a seed of life pattern in the crop fields as they traversed the journey back home.

45
A Final Encounter with Fergetcha Kundameanie

The pink and clear quartz front doors were barely clinging to their rusty hinges when the seven chakra princess sisters crossed the threshold into the castle. They burst upon the chaotic scene so abruptly that Fergetcha was knocked backward. It was just a moment later that Owl Woman flew in behind them, breathless and exhilarated.

The sisters screeched to a halt and stood wide-eyed, as if they had just seen the chaos in the castle for the very first time. They felt the fresh sting of waking up from their blind state of existence. Astonished, they slowly scanned their surroundings, wondering how long they had really lived in this decaying environment under the Kundameanie spell. Seeing most of the spiral staircase in a crumpled heap on the ground, the walls caved in, and all the windows broken, the seven chakra sisters felt sick.

Turning full circle, taking it all in, they finally spoke in unison. "Mom!? Dad!? What are you doing here!?"

This was one of the rare occasions that the Mother Queen and Father King descended from the penthouse into the castle. Their appearance meant that the seven sisters were about to experience another glorious celebration of elevation, or else they were going to get their butts kicked.

This time, it was the latter. The royal couple was in protective parental mode when they started shouting, "Where have you been? Look at this place! It's a disaster! You actually let that pathetic Kundameanie spell take hold of you? We thought you were much more energetically advanced in your evolutionary spiritual development than to stoop to those delusional levels of fear. Our castle life is in serious condition now. How do you plan to clean up this mess and get it well again?"

By this time Fergetcha had regained her balance. The shock of seeing the chakra sisters together made her choke and cough like a dirty coal factory spewing black smoke.

"Fergetcha Kundameanie, this is all your fault!" shouted Mother Queen. Being argumentative took its toll on her divine nature. She uncharacteristically fell into blame mode while taking a fighting stance with her fists flying, aiming right toward the trickster.

"Wait a second!" pleaded Owl Woman, forming a barrier between Mother Queen and Fergetcha. "This is all my fault. I promised to always guide and protect my godchildren, but I must have also fallen asleep. I missed my chance when I should have been more mindful."

Fergetcha and Owl Woman were now face-to-face for the first time. The hyper little MeeWee bird flitted around their heads. The royal protective parents were feeling the pull of gravity, which was far from their usual lofty heights. Everyone was breathing heavily with a tenacious determination to win the battle over the castle's future. The life force was stirring, and the intense energy filled the ground floor, causing the last of the support beams from the spiral staircase to crash down in an explosion of dust, rust, and disgust.

It took a long while before the sounds, smells, and smoke dissipated, settling everyone into the harsh reality of how the Kundameanie spell of forgetfulness was so destructive.

"This is all *your* fault, Queeny. You shouldn't have come to my land in the first place!" screamed Fergetcha.

"Well, someone had to transform your old paradigms, Fergetcha. You can't stop evolution no matter how hard you try! This disaster is all your fault, and your whole Kundameanie clan's fault, too!"

Suddenly, one harmonious tone of seven individual notes sang out, "Hold on, everybody! This is no one's fault! If we continue to blame ourselves or each other, then we will surely stay stuck in an unhealthy never-ending cycle of revenge and defeat. We have to take responsibility for what we have created here in the castle. Taking responsibility makes us free and will give the castle its life back again!"

"MeeWee. MeeWee. MeeWee!" squeaked the excited little bird as it flitted around the dilapidated castle's foyer.

Fergetcha couldn't believe what she was hearing. Mom and Dad were also taken aback at this unexpected proclamation from their daughters. Owl Woman was beaming with pride.

"Your old ways of dominance, control, and fear mongering are coming to an end, Fergetcha. The truth of your world revolves around conflict, competition, and harsh judgments. That doesn't work for us in the new world that we are creating by our choices. We are the seven chakra sisters, living in harmony now. We are one! And the whole of us is greater than our parts, as you can see. The days of Kundameanie attitudes of separation and divisiveness are over, Fergetcha. We are in our power again because we are in tune with our resilient inner spirit!"

Fergetcha was stunned into silence. Mother Queen and Father King were delighted when they heard this wise, unified voice, and Owl Woman fluffed herself and puffed her loving heart outward.

The enlightened cacophony continued. "Yes, we're back now. Fully awake and better than ever! As you can see, we have synergistically collaborated in our collective healing, which has evolved our energy into a coagulated conglomeration of cooperation!"

Fergetcha scratched her head, dumbfounded. "What?"

Mother Queen clarified, "I believe what the children are saying is that they are working together as a team now."

The seven sisters looked at each other in their usual way of understanding and winked at the idea that they were still called "children" after all they had been through. Aneeda stepped forward first. She walked in slow deliberate steps, feeling powerful and secure in her body again.

"I really need to thank you, Fergetcha Kundameanie. Because of your clever tactics to instill such unbearable, threatening energy, I was afraid of being lost in a big, scary world. I actually started to believe that I was of no value in this world, and that I couldn't trust myself or anyone else. But thanks to you, and the healing power of love from my chakra sisters, I finally remembered what I had already known: that I truly am safe wherever I am, and I really do belong to a wonderful supportive community. Just look at my incredible sister-tribe. I am abundant in family love!"

Fergetcha did not understand Aneeda's strength. She had never experienced anyone ever speaking so directly to her before. "Why would this stupid girl be thanking me?" she wondered.

Aneeda continued, "I thought I had forgotten my mother, or that she had abandoned and forgot about me. But thanks to you, I remembered that I have two mommies—my Divine Mother and my Earth Mother. They will never leave me, and I know now that I am never alone. I will always receive their endless soul-nourishing love. That is all I need!"

The Mother Queen and Father King smiled at each other and let Aneeda continue without interfering. Fergetcha was wheezing hard.

"I can and will take care of myself from now on because I know I do matter and I am worth it! I will eat nutritious foods from my abundant gardens again because I can trust my natural instincts, and I know I am secure because I have shelter over me, sort of," she said as she looked askance at the disheveled ruins of the castle around her.

"But, just so you know, Fergetcha," Aneeda continued with all her strength, "I'm a survivor and I have no fear of being the solid foundation for our castle, once we rebuild it. So, thank you, Fergetcha! I feel so fearless now I'm not even afraid to look you right in the eyes."

Fergetcha was frozen in her own fear of the unknown. Her familiar reactions of hiding, running away, or fighting back were stuck inside her like she had just swallowed a porcupine. She felt threatened to her core. Everyone had always looked away from her, never deliberately at her. How could Aneeda be this bold and fearless?

"Yes, Ms. Fergetcha, I do have a right to exist here in this miraculous physical form. My energy body is strong and my connection to the Spirit of Creation is solid. Iamone and Useeme, well, actually *all* of my sisters, will see that my connection to our Queenking will never be severed again."

Aneeda stood close to the Mother Queen and Father King, merging her emerging energy with theirs. "I may not know how I was born, Mom and Dad, but I remember why I am here now."

Turning back to the old haggard woman, Aneeda felt her power growing. "I forgot all of my blessings for a while, thanks to you, Fergetcha. But now that I have seen how harmful it is to live in fear, I choose to take full responsibility for myself to stay healthy and well, not only for my own sake but for the sake of all my sisters and our whole castle. I know that Iamone's spiritual energy keeps me connected to my ultimate divine truth, but I also know how much I love the experiences that a human body can have on the earth plane. My sisters Ivanna and Ahafta know what I'm talking about," said Aneeda, giving their hands an extra squeeze.

The MeeWee bird was doing double backflips with Owl Woman, and the chakra sisters' shoulders were shaking from laughter that came more from their bodies than their mouths.

"Now, I live in gratitude more than ever before, Fergetcha, because I will never forget that I really do have all that I need. There is no poverty for me. There is never a lack of anything! There is always abundant energy flowing to me, easily and effortlessly, from the earth, from my sisters, and from the universal energy of the Queenking!" She smiled broadly at her divine royal parents.

All of Aneeda's sisters surrounded her with cheers, almost drowning her out as she said with finality, "And there is plenty enough of everything, good and bad, for everyone! I have always known this, but I will never forget it thanks to you, Fergetcha Kundameanie!"

The Kundameanie spell was losing its potency, and Fergetcha's knees buckled under her. Ivanna jumped right in, not giving Fergetcha a moment to catch her breath.

"I also want to thank you, Fergetcha. Your little game was pretty harsh, kidnapping and drugging me! But because we finally understand your unfair Kundameanie rules, we have learned valuable lessons on how we can be more trusting of our own instincts in the future."

Fergetcha gagged as Ivanna continued, "Your 'spell' has shown me how sick I can be if I let my body's desires rule my life instead of allowing all my sisters to help me make good choices that will keep me healthy and happy. My relationships with all of my friends will be reciprocal and respectful again."

Ivanna's sisters clapped their hands in quick little movements of proper approval, encouraging her to continue.

"Your Kundameanie ways of harmful jealousy led me to a place of dark and shameful feelings. But I have learned how destructive it can be to feel guilty for simply being who I am naturally. Screw guilt! I honestly love myself and all of my feelings even more than I did before you showed up, Fergetcha! You helped me mature into a sensitive, emotional chakra woman who accepts and appreciates herself completely!"

Fergetcha covered her ears, not wanting to hear any more. She stumbled back against the staircase, almost falling over but catching herself in time when one more loose board under her foot fell through the floor of the castle.

"Oh, and as far as my vivacious sexuality goes," continued Ivanna without paying any attention to the echoing wood falling down, "thank you for the valuable lessons of self-restraint. Chastity has never felt so open, so pleasurable, or so much fun! My sisters have shown me that I can harness all my powerful creative energy into birthing a million different kinds of innovative projects for everyone to enjoy!"

Fergetcha winced when she heard Ivanna say this, fearing that her spell might not give the Kundameanie clan power over the castle on Mt. Iknowmenow after all. Her angry energy seared through her vengeful heart, raising her cortisol levels and sealing the fate of her chronic stress.

Ahafta stood tall with her third floor confidence and when she spoke her sisters could almost see flames coming out of her mouth, dripping like golden honey onto her words.

"You once asked me 'Who do you think you are?' Well, I'll tell you, Fergetcha. I am me, magnificent just as I am! You've taught me that it's impossible for me to be obedient to anything other than my own gut feelings and highest intuition. I follow my own confident guidance, no one else's. I trust and believe in myself and I don't need to defend myself to anyone anymore."

"MeeWee. MeeWee. MeeWee." came the familiar reminder.

"Oh yes," answered Ahafta's call from the mighty bird, "as for my sisters and me, we work together as one hot, courageous team, each of us doing what we do best to help each other. I know exactly how I fit into the mix to keep everyone motivated, without burning myself out! Nothing and no one can stop us from manifesting our dreams, especially you, Fergetcha!"

The seven chakra princess sisters were gaining power in their collective voice, but before they spoke this time, Ahluvya reminded them again about compassion. "Fergetcha, we are aware of our empathic gifts now more than ever, because of you. We want you to know that we can feel the deep pain that you've lived with for eons. We know how your body aches every day from this intense stress that you keep creating for yourself. We know what it feels like to be so depressed that you lose all your energy and desire to live. We know the debilitating thoughts and negative self-talk that have been circulating in your mind, and how that has caused your disillusioned mental state and emotional dysfunction. We know that you are really very afraid of everything and you feel completely separated from the Great Creative Force of Universal Love. And that's why you do what you do."

Fergetcha snarled. She was the one squirming this time. She was so good at trickery and avoiding direct conversation that being addressed this honestly by the seven sisters caused her to shake inside. No one had ever spoken to her about how she might actually be feeling before, much less cared.

"Fergetcha," said Ahluvya, being the most forthright with her immense compassion, "we know that you have never felt love before, have you? You have never been recognized or validated or noticed by anyone, ever, and you have never loved yourself because of that. We know you have never known what it feels like to love another. You have no concept of love—how to give it or how to receive it."

"Oh, just go away! Leave me alone!" Fergetcha's face twisted as the bizarre sensation of salty tears filled her eyes, dripped down her wrinkled cheeks, and touched the corners of her dry, cracked lips.

"We can hear your deep inner cries of loneliness, Fergetcha, because you have never known how to express love before," said Singya, balancing her listening skills with honest speaking. "We know that underneath your mean demeanor, there is a very sad woman who has always been afraid to live fully. You've never felt comfortable with simply speaking your gentle truth, have you? We have great sympathy for your pain and heartache, Fergetcha. That makes us feel very sad for your fragile existence."

"Noooo!" screamed Fergetcha. "Shut up! I don't want your sympathy."

"We don't mean to cause you further pain, dear soul," said Useeme, now in her right mind. Her intuitive senses were also filled with the same compassion that flowed through all of her sisters. "We just wanted you to know that we do understand how it's been for you. We see you! If you knew better, you'd *do* better! But no one ever told you there was another way to live. We want you to know that we love you for all the sacrifices you have made to help us see both sides of life."

"What? Stop it! Don't say these things . . . leave me alone!" Ferget-cha moaned, not knowing how to exist in a place where this strange kind of love was flowing toward her so freely.

"Every thought you've ever had about a hard and unfair life has come to pass for you and is the only reality you have known, Fergetcha. You created your own sad circumstances of despair by the very thoughts you've been thinking because no one showed you any other possibility," said Useeme, who was fully aware of all the synapses that were firing in her brain as she spoke. "We know how important it is to constantly be mindful of every thought we think, so we will think lovingly of you from now on, in gratitude for the lessons we've learned from you."

The collective chorus of the seven sisters' voices hummed in harmony with Iamone's vibration as she spoke, "Yes, isn't it wonderful?! You have energized our joy! We are awake now with a simple change of attitude! We don't blame you, Fergetcha. We know you were here to test our truest belief in ourselves. You've helped us see how we are able to express the many facets of light that we are. You've shown us how we can choose to either selfishly destroy life or lovingly create life. Because of your old Kundameanie tradition of death and destruction, we have learned that the God Consciousness of Living Energy within our castle is very, very precious, and we will never take it for granted again."

"Oh no . . . I hate you . . . I can't take anymore . . ." was all that the distraught, hollow-eyed woman could muster up. Fergetcha was deflated, depleted, debilitated, and exhausted from centuries of old, worn-out ideas and nonproductive actions.

Owl Woman, the silent MeeWee bird, and the royal parents were compassionate witnesses to what came next.

Like a brilliant diamond with multiple facets and colors, the seven chakra sisters encompassed Fergetcha Kundameanie in a soft, swirling rainbow of energy. Spinning around the pathetic character who felt too wretched and helpless to react, they collectively knew their intention of simply loving the old consciousness into something new. They merged into one radiant being of white light with the same vibration that entered through Iamone's skylights.

"We will never forget you, Fergetcha, and we are grateful for all you have taught us and done for us. Before you leave, we want you to know that we forgive you for not knowing a better way. It's not your fault. No one is to blame for innocent ignorance."

The Kundameanie legend was so entrenched with grim attitudes that the idea of anyone forgiving her was simply never imagined. Fergetcha was now surrounded, feeling astounded by seven chakra princess sisters who were beaming the most unusual energies of kindness, compassion, understanding, forgiveness, and unconditional love. She felt herself drop her guard for one quick moment, which opened the doorway to vulnerability and transformation, which Fergetcha had managed to avoid for eons.

The seven chakra sisters unleashed their greatest loving and merciful voices when they asked, "Fergetcha, will you please forgive us for not bringing healing and peace to you before now? You've been in darkness for such a long time that we wanted to share our light and infinite love with you as you go."

In that moment, a whirlwind of air currents blasted through the open walls of the castle. Within the elevated gusts, as if the universe had exhaled a multitude of assistance, all the summoned spirit guides, angels, archangels, ascended masters, wisdom sages, alchemists, and evolved self-actualized light beings suddenly appeared on the ground floor of the crumbling crystal castle.

There was a long hush before anyone spoke. "Well," said Mother Queen, as if her late dinner guests had finally arrived, "timing is everything, isn't it?"

The seven chakra princess sisters laughed lightheartedly, feeling gratitude for the abundance of spiritual helpers who were around them.

"Apparently, the Beautiful Ones have already managed to work this out on their own!" boasted Owl Woman.

Their favorite cousin, Oimalive Fundalini, arrived with an entourage of avatars. She brought the chakra sisters close to her at the base of the column of light, and in an instant they apprehended the magnitude of the force that would rebuild, heal, and stabilize the castle.

Everyone watched as electromagnetic waves of energy began to increase the spinning rainbow of color, light, sound, and vibration on the ground floor where the assembly was gathered. The seven chakra sisters were breathing in long, deep inhalations, exhaling healing sounds, and unleashing their massive and extraordinary creative potential, fueled by love. They could only give away that which they knew they already had within themselves.

The seven sisters wrapped their luminous body around Fergetcha with their powerful intentions to save the castle and reverse the Kundameanie spell completely. For the first time, they felt fully developed enough to directly use the radiant column of white light and its life-giving energy. As the seven chakra sisters began to lift Fergetcha Kundameanie into the column of light, they were escorted by a host of angels and other helpers who were eager to assist. Their swirling ascension rose one floor at a time, moving from the ground floor up to the skylights on Iamone's top floor.

Through the clear white tornado of activity, each sister merged her individual thoughts of encouragement, blessings, and, most of all, forgiveness and love to Fergetcha.

"You are safe and secure, Fergetcha. There is nothing to fear anymore. All of your needs will be met at your next destination of a higher, unified consciousness," promised Aneeda.

Rising to the second floor, Ivanna exclaimed, "You are free to effortlessly dance and move into pleasure now, Fergetcha! In your new level of living, may all your desires serve you and your new relationships with respect."

They could see sunlight sparkling off the last of the crystal shards that remained intact on the castle walls. As they ascended to the third floor in the column of light, Ahafta asserted, "Have courage on your firewalk of transformation, old friend. I believe in your true power to manifest goodness. I am optimistic about your future."

Swirling higher and faster now, Fergetcha began to feel an urge to let go of her tightly gripped body. In the midst of their spinning on the fourth floor, Ahluvya gave her a hug and whispered, "You are always being embraced by an endless supply of love, Fergetcha. It will be easy for you to be loving to yourself and to others in your next home. May your heart expand easily and effortlessly, so you can accept all things within the vast space of love within you."

Fergetcha could not recall if she had ever been hugged before. She felt a strange distancing from her ancient Kundameanie family with their condemning ideologies, and a new sensation of freedom. For once she did not fight the energy that was circulating around her at such elevated speeds.

On the fifth floor, beautiful harmonies rushed through sound tunnels, making Singya's vocal vibrations sing like delicate tingsha bells tinkling. "You are right, Fergetcha, I will never forget you. May you also remember how important your voice will be in your new awareness, where you will speak your truth with kindness, uplifting everyone you meet."

Fergetcha had no idea where they were taking her and didn't have the wherewithal to ask. She was so enveloped in the powerful light and energy that was being emitted by the seven sisters that she could barely breathe.

Rising even higher now, they all floated up to the sixth floor together. The energy in the column of light circulated around them at even faster speeds now. Useeme and Fergetcha looked into one another's eyes and neither blinked. "You will soon see things very clearly with a much higher perspective, Fergetcha. Now your incredibly clever imagination and intelligence will work toward helping people instead of harming them."

A host of angels accompanied the spiraling vortex of chakra sisters as they lifted Fergetcha from the column of light directly to the seventh floor. Iridescent light beams reflected from within Iamone's open space, bouncing ultraviolet fragments of wisdom through their gyrating wheel of energy.

Barely audible as she conveyed thoughts more than a spoken voice, Iamone transmitted her message in a tone that was dreamy and melodic, "It has only been your fears that blinded you from this light, Fergetcha. Fear cannot exist in the midst of this unlimited love. You can finally be free if you are willing to receive and feel the peace that awaits you."

Iamone's skylights were wide open, and the whole bundle of energy lifted up and out, merging their colors into one magnificent ball of radiant vibration. They swirled Fergetcha into the multidimensional field of her Kundameanie heritage where the power of love completely dissolved the ancient lineage of forgetfulness.

"You are a divine being, receiving higher thoughts from the one universal mind. In this unified field, you will continue to learn knowledge from the Source of all as you evolve, Fergetcha. Enjoy the journey! You are guided by pure consciousness now."

The soul of Fergetcha was remembering its own divine spark again, and the seven chakra sisters knew it was time to release her into the great beyond, leaving them free to return to Mt. Iknowmenow in peace and solidarity.

"Goodbye, Fergetcha Kundameanie! The loving universe will take care of you from this point forward until you learn how to take care of yourself with the same love. Remember, it's all within you!"

With that, Fergetcha was whorled into a beautiful world she never could have imagined, championed by an entourage of angelic protectors. She was blending into the one-mind-soul-universal-power-of-love in boundless space. She was filled with the sweetness of music, joy, and inspiration, feeling lighter and freer as she spun through the light that carried her beyond limitations. The Kundameanie spell was lifted from the earth below.

Fergetcha reverberated in the vibrations of strange and amazing names she had never heard before, all speaking in her mind at once: Godmatrixuniverse Hashembuddhajesussophia Krishnamohammedghandiji Starseedsunlight Greatspiritallaharucha Christedlordpeacejoy Kwanyingaialove Pachamamafathertime. Everything flowed together. Boundaries blurred until there was no separation anymore. Nothing made sense, and yet she felt curiously connected to this extraordinary experience of peace by being one with everything.

Transcending eons of the Kundameanie's old consciousness of self-centered divisiveness, Fergetcha's sheaths of ignorance peeled away as she was lifted higher and higher into a vast space of new potential and learning opportunities. She was never seen in Thisismeville again.

46

One More
Important Choice
for the
7 Chakra Sisters

The seven chakra sisters hovered, intermingling their energy high over their parents' penthouse for a while, basking in the oneness and joy they were experiencing. They were completely free from the Kundameanie spell, undistracted, unaffected, and uninvolved with any illusions on the material plane. They were no longer attached to the physical world. At this point of union, they knew they would continue to grow and evolve together by choice, not by chance.

The seven princess sisters had never been inside the penthouse before, as their main domain was to maintain the crystal castle. The Queenking opened the doors and invited their collective brilliant light inside.

Immediately, they were spiritually illuminated within the full spectrum of mystical experience. In this timeless dimension of extraordinary reality, they instantly knew all that the Tribe of All-Knowing had known since the beginning of the beginning. The seven chakra sisters were healed, whole, and complete as One Being.

They enjoyed floating in this serene and peaceful union with the divine universe. They were dissolving and evolving simultaneously. Their radiant ball of light remained motionless and silent for an endless time.

However, their impulsive nature to always move and explore something new was urging them to vibrate their eternal energy. Someone chose to splinter off just a bit. Iamone was the first. She uttered something to herself which translated into the one pure consciousness of Sublime Intelligence where all of the sisters were integrated into the Original One Thought of the One Mind of the One Heart of the One Source of One Love.

Choosing to shift out of her ineffable state, Iamone finally said to her sisters, "We could remain forever in the penthouse with our Queenking, staying perpetually immersed in this bliss of enlightenment . . . or we can consciously choose to go back to our beloved crystal castle and clean up the place before we entitle ourselves to an everlasting state of nirvana."

Upon hearing that, a subtle sliver of a shiver started stirring, suddenly stimulating their light and rippling through the one sphere of transcendent energy that pulsed in the room.

Aneeda remembered how much she loved her Mother Earth and all things physical. Ivanna remembered how the pleasures of emotions and the senses made her feel so alive. Ahafta remembered that there were fires to be lit and dreams to be manifested. Ahluvya remembered the power of love and how it brought compassion and respect to everyone she encountered. Singya remembered how her soulful inner sounds could create harmony, beauty, and truth in the world. Useeme remembered how her intuitive visions had the power to evolve the realm of imagination toward the realization of all intentions and new possibilities. Iamone didn't have to remember anything. She always knew what she always knew as the ultimate reality.

Together, the seven chakra sisters remembered it was their job to co-create as one synergistic team, to evolve, have fun, and enliven a new, expanding consciousness within humanity.

"Sisters, we have work to do. Agreed?"

"You bet."

"And once our castle has been rebuilt and polished clean,"

"and Mt. Iknowmenow is standing tall again,"

"with an indestructible foundation of love holding it up,"

"then we will celebrate life with another grand festival for everyone in the entire queendom!" Their vibrational frequencies were quivering with the energy of pure joy.

"Sounds fantastic, sisters! But what if . . ." Iamone planted one more tiny seed of an evolutionary thought before they left the penthouse. "What if in our reconstruction we found a way to make our new castle stronger, more stable, and mobile? What if we could detach it from the mountainside and go out on the road to explore the big world beyond Thisismeville?"

"Yeah! What if we could adventure forth into a larger territory and co-create a new ThisisWEville?!"

"Yes, *lots* of little ThisisWEville villages, where we will share what we have learned, showing people how to be self-reliant, take responsibility for their lives and never again be victims of their circumstances."

"We, sisters, *we*—not they or us, theirs or ours, them or me—*we*. We will co-create communities where everyone stops the idea of separation."

"Just like us, being one!"

"Then selfishness will end, and everyone will plant seeds of peace!"

The sisters were ready, assured with more hope and excitement than ever.

Owl Woman and the sapphire-colored MeeWee bird were perched high on the mountainside, waiting patiently for the princesses to come back to earth. Leaping off the precipice together, they sped toward the front door of the castle where Owl Woman skidded to a stop. Keeping her large wing-arms open, she stood like a benevolent guard, halting the seven chakra sisters before they entered.

"Welcome home, my bliss-filled babies!" she said in her imitable fashion of being slightly behind the wave.

"Owl Woman, we love you! Thank you for our healing!" they said, swarming their guardian with hugs of appreciation.

"I love you too, dear Beautiful Ones. Now, before you go out to create a whole new world, it is important to acknowledge the understanding in every experience. I have one very important question for you: what have you learned about this grand adventure?"

The girls looked at each other and roared with laughter, knowing that there was no need to put their enlightened understanding into words. But they indulged Owl Woman's inquiry and responded by giving their beloved teacher a chance to answer her own question. "Why, we can't think of how to phrase it, Owl Woman. Will you give us a hint?"

Standing a bit taller with both pride and humility, Owl Woman didn't hesitate to take the stage. "Well," she said, clearing her throat, "since you have asked, thank you. Firstly, you have learned to remember who you are, directly from the queen of forgetfulness herself. How ironic."

The sisters nodded in agreement.

"And second, you have learned about true forgiveness. It took a lot of guts to do what you did for Fergetcha Kundameanie."

Feeling no need to respond or explain how they were just doing the spiritually natural and loving thing to do, the seven chakra sisters started humming in harmony together, allowing Owl Woman time to collect her thoughts.

"Well, dear Beautiful Ones, this is what else we have learned," Owl Woman spoke as one with the sisters, who were now leaning forward, listening intently for her never-ending words of wisdom. "Our experiences have given us new co-creative abilities that carry new responsibilities. We must never again be victims of the circumstances around us."

The chakra siblings gave each other a questioning glance, asking themselves, "didn't we already talk about this?" As usual, the godmother was one breath short of a tie.

"It starts right inside of us. And that means we must stop fighting within our own hearts and minds. We must stop fighting with our neighbors, our co-workers, our parents, and our children. We must stop judging, comparing, and blaming. We must stop fighting with ourselves!"

The seven chakra sisters knew all of this but patiently let the ancient guardian speak her piece.

"We have learned that we must teach others how they must stop drawing lines in the sand, and stop wanting one particular outcome to manifest. We must help others to stop their inside battles of staying small, of feeling unworthy, of causing wars! We must show them how to stop their faulty thinking and behaving. You are the seven chakra sisters, the team of united energies who must lead the way and help evolve Consciousness!"

Owl Woman's voice faded in their minds. The princess sisters were getting restless and didn't want to linger in a lecture any longer, no matter how well meaning it was. Their energy was fully charged and they felt like thoroughbreds waiting for the gates to open. They were anxious to rebuild the castle and move forward with their new life of infinite possibilities.

Honoring their beloved teacher with appreciation but standing in their own enlightened self-authority, they spoke up. "Yes, Owl Woman, thank you for the lessons of what we must stop doing. But remember, the most important thing we must *never* stop doing is to keep growing and keep going! So let's get on with it, right now!"

Surprised at their adorable boldness, Owl Woman grinned. She grabbed up the little MeeWee bird along with those bratty septuplets and blasted off toward the stars. Twirling and swirling their collective energies together, they ascended, leaving an echo of joyous laughter settling like smoke rings over Mt. Iknowmenow. *Aneeda . . . Ivanna . . . Ahafta . . . Ahluvya . . . Singya . . . Useeme . . . Iamone.*

It was the end . . . and the beginning.

Glossary

Chakra—"shock-ra" or "chock-ra"—a spinning wheel of energy that corresponds to one's spiritual consciousness. The energy that flows into and out of these spinning portals (from the universe, environment, food, water, air, thoughts, beliefs, and attitudes) is an exchange of information that affects the physical, emotional, and psychological aspects of development. There are seven major chakras, located near and corresponding to the endocrine system of a human body, spanning from the base of the spine to the top of the head:

- 1st chakra: the root chakra—adrenals—located between the anus and sexual organs
- 2nd chakra: the sacral chakra—ovaries/testes, reproductive glands, kidneys, bladder—located below the navel
- 3rd chakra: the solar plexus chakra—pancreas/spleen—located above the navel in the solar plexus region
- 4th chakra: the heart chakra—heart/thymus glands—located in the center of the chest at the heart level
- 5th chakra: the throat chakra—thyroid/ parathyroid glands—located at the larynx
- 6th chakra: the brow chakra—pineal/pituitary gland (the "boss" of the endocrine system)—located at the middle of the forehead
- 7th chakra: the crown chakra—pituitary/pineal gland—located at the top-center of the head

The Seven Chakra Sisters and Their Significance

Name	Pronunciation	Chakra	Location	Color	Element	Qualities
Aneeda	"uh-*need*-uh" (I need a)	1st	root	red	earth	basic needs, foundation, support, safety, trust, physical health, fight or flight, groundedness, need to belong
Ivanna	"eye-*vahn*-nah" (I want a)	2nd	sacral	orange	water	desires, pleasure, duality, sensuality, emotions, relationships, wants to enjoy everything
Ahafta	"ah-*haf*-tah" (I have to)	3rd	solar plexus	yellow	fire	personal power, self-esteem, confidence, self-authority, motivation, metabolism/digestion, has to move/transform energy
Ahluvya	"ah-*love*-ya" (I love you	4th	heart	green	air	breath, all-inclusive, unconditional love, empathy, compassion
Singya	"*sing*-yah" (sing, you!)	5th	throat	sky blue/ turquoise	sound	harmony, creative and spiritual expression, listening to the intuitive voice
Useeme	"you-*see*-me" (you see me)	6th	brow/ third eye	indigo	light/ insight	imagination, thought, visionary/inner vision, intuition, intelligence, sees everything from a higher perspective
Iamone	"*eye*-ah-moan" (I am one)	7th	crown	violet/ gold/ white	knowing	higher mind, soul purpose, universal consciousness, one with all, spirituality, self-actualization, inner authority, enlightenment, wisdom

Aunt Ida and Uncle Pingala—an anthropomorphized version of the spiral staircase. They are the personalities of the *Ida* (female, cool, moon) and *Pingala* (male, hot, sun) nadis. A *nadi* literally means "river," and in traditional Indian medicine it refers to a channel for the flow of spiritual consciousness. Ida runs on the left side of the spinal column and corresponds to the left side of the brain. Pingala runs on the right side. They crisscross the *Sushumna* at each chakra point on an upward path and converge at the nose level, igniting light at the third eye.

Ceremonial Field—symbolic of the subconscious state of mind during a meditation or a shamanic experience where one's consciousness is transported to spiritual realms of new visions, ideas, and possibilities. The chakra sisters would "leave their body" of the castle, first going within and then journeying outward to the open field of pure potential during a sacred ceremony. Healing takes place from within, once a new understanding is experienced.

Column of Light—represents the Sushumna nadi, a channel for the Kundalini flow of consciousness. It is the center channel that runs subtle, spiritual energy up the spine. Located in the middle of the ida and pingala nadis, it is the point of connection between the cosmos (crown chakra "Iamone") and the earth (root chakra "Aneeda") through the human physical body.

Crystal Castle—represents the human body, whose physical, emotional, mental, and spiritual health is affected by the health of the chakras concerning security, relationships, personal power, love, creative expression, intuition, and Higher Self–awareness. Each floor corresponds to the location, bodily organs, and specific personality traits of the chakra sisters (see chart)

Fergetcha Kundameanie—"fer-*get*-cha coon-dah-*mean*-ie"— represents an egoic state of lower consciousness with old paradigms of greed, ignorance, fear, lack, and separation. Fergetcha represents forgetting one's connection to Spirit, causing the mental and emotional stress factors that create human illness and disease. Kundameanie is the opposite of Fundalini, who is life-giving. Kundameanie energy lacks integrity, is limiting, divisive, and destructive—and no fun at all.

Flower of Insight—located in a small vase inside the Insight Chamber, the elixir from the Flower of Insight represents the hormone molecule DMT (dimethyltryptamine), a psychedelic compound found in plant and animal (mammal) life that might be produced by the pineal gland. Sometimes referred to as the essence of Soul, or the "spirit gland/molecule" by various mystery schools, DMT is a naturally occurring molecule that helps one explore metaphysical mystical states, spiritual consciousness, and higher transcendent levels of reality.

Fundalini—"fun-da-*leeni*"—this story's fun version of Kundalini, which is the life energy that rises in the subtle body (the energetic level of our being) and awakens consciousness. *Kundalini* is a Sanskrit term which means "serpent power" or "that which is coiled." In Hindu mythology, the goddess Kundalini rests as a coiled snake that can stir and rise up to open and energize each chakra when spiritually aroused. When activated, Kundalini energy clears away the ego's attachments and helps us recognize our full human potential and ultimately, unification with the Divine. Controlled breathing activates the process and enlivens a person with vitality, a strong immune system, inner peace, relief from physical ailments, feelings of well being, and overall bliss.

Insight Chamber—represents the deep center of the brain where the singular pineal gland is located. Considered a mysterious and holy inner chamber like that of ancient temples where the Eternal One can be reached. It is significant in mystical awakening or enlightenment, clairvoyant perception, and higher states of consciousness. The pineal gland is photosensitive, about the size of a grain of rice, and is shaped like a pine cone, (hence its name and association with the third eye). The gland represents evolution's earlier function of photoreception. It helps set our natural circadian rhythms by receiving light signals. Useeme's element is light.

MeeWee Bird—represents the concept of remembering a higher order of living with teamwork, cooperation, and collaboration, moving from self-centered isolationism to inclusiveness, from ego (me) to essence (spiritual truth and unity with all—"we").

Mt. Iknowmenow—"Mount I-*know*-me-now"—the earthbound base of support for the crystal castle, representing the "ground on which we stand."

Oimalive—"oh-*I'm*-alive!"—her name represents the active life energy that ignites the Kundalini, awakening humans to feel alive, vital, healthy, and happy—physically, mentally, emotionally, and spiritually (see Fundalini).

Owl Woman—represents one's inner wisdom as a wise elder, godmother, kindly grandmother, guardian angel, spiritual mentor, or loyal companion who teaches and guides with enthusiasm and unconditional love. She shapeshifts from having human attributes to mythical powers.

Penthouse—represents a possible eighth chakra located a few inches above the head—a transpersonal point beyond the physical body, and a portal between the brain, higher mind, and the cosmos.

Queenking—"queen-king"—an anthropomorphized version of Universal Intelligence or God Consciousness, the highest electromagnetic frequency or vibration. The Queenking represents the ultimate awakened state of oneness, no longer in duality, and the merging of feminine and masculine energies.

Shapeshifter—one who can transform from human form to animal or bird form and vice versa.

Spiral Staircases—represent the energy pathways that balance the ida and pingala so the sleeping serpent Kundalini can awaken, uncoil itself from the base of the spine, and rise up the column of light (Sushumna nadi), bringing enlightenment and liberation. It can also represent the shape of the double helix of human DNA. The caduceus of Western medicine is a depiction of the two serpents coiling upward and around the Sushumna.

Thisismeville—"this-is-*me*-ville"—represents the town, individuals, family, friends, and community. Each person in Thisismeville also has his or her own crystal castle, (a physical body composed of seven main chakras) of which they may or may not be aware.

ThisisWEville—"this-is-*we*-ville"—represents a co-creative community of family, friends, co-workers, etc. who live in a consciousness of cooperation and unity while respecting individual differences.

About the Author

Victoria Fane

Linda Linker Rosenthal is the founder and creative director of Insight Out Visionary Healing Arts Center. She is a writer, teacher, healer, recording artist, ordained minister, and a graduate of Delphi University with doctorate degrees in metaphysical healing and transpersonal psychology. Her training in intuitive journaling, chakra studies, meditation, Reiki, energy medicine, aromatherapy, and sound healing has been the foundation for her private practice as a transformational healer. Linda facilitates annual Healing Retreats: The Midwest Reiki Convergence, Women's Wisdom Circles, Spiritual Gatherings, and Community Reiki Healing Sanctuaries. Her greatest understanding of living an honest spiritual life continues to come from being mom to three grown children and grandmother of a granddaughter. This is her first book.

Visit Linda at *www.lindalinkerrosenthal.com*